CAUSES AND CURES

OF

POVERTY

By

J. Paul Reno

Pastor and Author

Causes and Cures of Poverty

Copyrighted © by Pastor Paul Reno
Hagerstown, MD
January, 2016

ISBN 978-0-9962591-9-4

Published by
Blessed Hope Publishers
Hagerstown, Md.

Publishing and Formatting Assisted by
The Old Paths Publications
142 Gold Flume Way
Cleveland, GA 30528
Web address: www.theoldpathspublications.com
Email address: TOP@theoldpathspublications.com

All Scripture quotations in this book are taken from the King James Version of the Bible.

"All scripture is given by inspiration of God, and is profitable for doctrine, for reproof, for correction, for instruction in righteousness.

That the man of God may be perfect, throughly furnished unto all good works."

(II Tim. 3:16, 17)

DEDICATION

Dedicated to my Sunday School teachers, especially Paul Pontus, who taught me that the Bible had the answers to all questions of life, and these answers were to be trusted implicitly even if the world disagreed.

Further, I dedicate this to all Sunday School teachers who faithfully instruct their students to fully trust the pure words of God above all other authorities.

Pastor J. Paul Reno
January, 2016

TABLE OF CONTENTS

DEDICATION 3
TABLE OF CONTENTS 5
PREFACE 7
CHAPTER 1: CAUSES AND CURES OF POVERTY 9
   WHAT IS POVERTY? 9
   POVERTY IS A SPIRITUAL ISSUE 9
   GOD WANTS YOU TO PROSPER 9
   THE CAUSES OF POVERTY 10
   SATAN DECEIVES IN THE REALM OF FINANCES 11
   WILLINGLY CHOOSING POVERTY? 11
   POVERTY IS A PART OF LIVING ON EARTH 12
   POVERTY IS A RESULT OF CHOICES 12
   LEARNING TO BE CONTENT 13
   THE SIGNIFICANCE OF INCOME AMOUNTS 14
   SCRIPTURE ASKS US TO CONSIDER THE CAUSE OF THE POOR 15
   A VICIOUS CYCLE 16
   THE BIBLE HAS A FINANCIAL PHILOSOPHY 16
   POOR PEOPLE DON'T JUST HAPPEN 17
   GOD'S RULES WORK 18
CHAPTER 2: DOING BUSINESS WITH GREEDY PEOPLE ... 21
   WHAT IS THE CURE? 22
CHAPTER 3: SLEEPING TOO MUCH 23
CHAPTER 4: TRAVELING 25
   WHAT IS THE CURE? 26
CHAPTER 5: LOOSE MORAL LIVING 27
   WHAT IS THE CURE? 29
CHAPTER 6: LIVING WICKEDLY 31
   WHAT IS THE CURE? 32
CHAPTER 7: DEALING WITH A SLACK HAND 35
   WHAT IS THE CURE? 35
CHAPTER 8: LACK OF DEFENSE OR PROTECTION 39
   WHAT IS THE CURE? 40
CHAPTER 9: STINGINESS IN GIVING 41
   WHAT IS THE CURE? 42
CHAPTER 10: WEALTH GOTTEN BY VANITY 43
   WHAT IS THE CURE? 44

CHAPTER 11: REFUSING INSTRUCTION 49
   WHAT IS THE CURE? 50
CHAPTER 12: TALK OF THE LIPS – NO LABOR 53
   WHAT IS THE CURE? 54
CHAPTER 13: WASTEFULNESS 59
   A PERSON WHO IS WASTEFUL. 59
   WHAT IS THE CURE? 60
CHAPTER 14: SLOTHFULNESS 63
   WHAT IS THE CURE? 69
CHAPTER 15: IGNORING THE NEEDS OF THE POOR 71
   WHAT IS THE CURE? 71
CHAPTER 16: LOVE OF PLEASURE 75
   WHAT IS THE CURE? 76
CHAPTER 17: SPENDING IT UP 77
   WHAT IS THE CURE? 79
CHAPTER 18: BORROWING MONEY 81
   WHAT IS THE CURE? 83
CHAPTER 19: OPPRESSION OF THE POOR 87
   WHAT IS THE CURE? 89
CHAPTER 20: GIVING GIFTS TO THE RICH 91
   WHAT IS THE CURE? 91
CHAPTER 21: DRUNKENNESS 93
   WHAT IS THE CURE? 96
CHAPTER 22: GLUTTONY 99
   WHAT IS THE CURE? 100
CHAPTER 23: VAIN FRIENDS 101
   WHAT IS THE CURE? 102
CHAPTER 24: GET RICH QUICK SCHEMES 103
   WHAT IS THE CURE? 105
CHAPTER 25: CONCLUSION 107
INDEX OF WORDS AND PHRASES 111
ABOUT THE AUTHOR 115

PREFACE

As I grew up, it seemed that the only Bible teaching I heard on the subject of money had to do with giving. Imagine my surprise to read much in my Bible regarding a variety of other aspects: poverty, savings, investments, business, wills, estates, debt and far more.

In college, Professor Sinclair further opened my mind to Bible principles pertaining to money. Now, over 50 years later, I present some of what I have found clearly taught in God's Word. May these thoughts open our minds to search diligently to find God's answers to the financial issues we face.

Pastor J. Paul Reno
January, 2016

CHAPTER 1

CAUSES AND CURES OF POVERTY

WHAT IS POVERTY?

Poverty is not a definite condition, rather it is an issue of degree. We are all poor to some degree or another, just as we are all rich to some degree. Some of us have greater degrees of poverty and lesser degrees of wealth.

POVERTY IS A SPIRITUAL ISSUE

I am convinced this is a real spiritual issue, though I know there are many people that preach a "Health-and-Wealth Gospel" as if that was all there is to it. If that is all that you are interested in, then you have made an idol of health and become covetous over wealth. There is danger in a health and wealth gospel, but there is also danger in those that care nothing about their health and are foolish in the matter of their wealth.

GOD WANTS YOU TO PROSPER

Those two extremes are both out of balance with the Word of God. In III John, the Apostle John wrote to Gaius that he wished that he might prosper and be in health, even as his soul prospered. That would be an insult to some people because by saying that you would be wishing they were broke and dead. These are vital issues for us to consider that have some effects spiritually and Biblically on our life and our testimony before a lost and dying world.

Let's begin by looking at **Matthew 26:6-11**. It says,

> "Now when Jesus was in Bethany, in the house of Simon the leper, There came unto him a woman

having an alabaster box of very precious ointment, and poured it on his head, as he sat at meat. But when his disciples saw it, they had indignation, saying, To what purpose is this waste? For this ointment might have been sold for much, and given to the poor. When Jesus understood it, he said unto them, Why trouble ye the woman? for she hath wrought a good work upon me. For ye have the poor always with you; but me ye have not always."

THE CAUSES OF POVERTY

There is such a thing recognized Biblically as "poverty" and the Bible is quite precise in spelling out the causes of it. Some causes are beyond our control. For example, sickness can cause poverty. There was a woman in the New Testament that had spent all that she had on doctors but was not any better **(Mark 5:25-29)**. Death can bring poverty to a family, particularly when it hits the man of the house before there is any chance for finances to be set aside. Taxes can bring poverty. Some governments try to make their people poor by taxing and manipulation. Disasters, such as earthquakes or fires that burn out businesses, can bring poverty. Weather can bring poverty for farmers. They can lose what they have worked years for because of one bad season. Some other examples of causes of poverty are handicaps, war, bad economy, lack of opportunity, or the judgment of God on a people. These are some things that we don't control.

There are far more causes of poverty that we do control than those which we can't do anything about. These are the ones that I want to deal with. We would like to blame everything on what we cannot control, but we need to face that at least part of our poverty is self-induced and brought upon ourselves by ignorance of the laws of God.

CHAPTER 1: CAUSES AND CURES OF POVERTY

SATAN DECEIVES IN THE REALM OF FINANCES

I also believe Satan has deceived the thinking of Christians in the realm of finances, so as to bind up the children of God financially. This, in turn, causes a lack of free money for God's program. There was a time when there was adequate money among the people of God to buy a piece of ground, build a building for a Christian college or new church, or send a missionary out within a couple of months of when he was ready. In the area of missions now it takes years before believers can bind together to even think about promising enough to send someone to the field. There are a number of reasons for this, but I believe Satan has deceived our thinking and confused the saints, getting them into a state of poverty so that they are not able to operate according to God's plan for meeting needs.

WILLINGLY CHOOSING POVERTY?

Further, many Christians that have not been deceived have ignorantly or even willingly chosen poverty. Some believers and churches think that the poorer you are the more spiritual you are. I am convinced that some churches feel that it is their obligation to keep their members financially strapped, bound up, behind on their bills and feeling guilty if they ever can get two nickels to rub together in their pocket before they get the next paycheck. They say, "You can wait to pay your bills while the church pays hers."

Taking vows of poverty does not make a person spiritual. If God leads someone to do that, fine. But I do not believe that Abraham was wicked when he had all those servants, possessions, and jobs for those servants. Neither do I believe that David was a wicked sinner when he was able to lay aside millions and millions of dollars worth of gold and silver to build the temple. I don't believe that Solomon was in deep sin when he was able to roll in the millions of dollars every year, adding to his income and the treasure house for building to the glory of the God that he worshipped. Neither do I believe that Job was wicked when he was blessed of God and given double what he used to have. Remember, Job was given all those things by God. God sometimes finds a saint that He can trust and then He prospers them.

POVERTY IS A PART OF LIVING ON EARTH

The Biblical principle is that the *"poor ye have always with you"* (**Matthew 26:11**). Poverty is a permanent part of living here on earth. You can't eradicate poverty. The richest government with the finest and strongest economy in the world has just about gone bankrupt, nearly destroying its' economy trying to prove that Jesus was wrong on this verse when it had a war on poverty. By the way – we lost. Poverty is still here.

I can remember as a boy when we established the minimum wage of 60¢ an hour to get rid of poverty! You can laugh now, but with the present minimum wage at $10.00 an hour in some places in 2016, we still have poverty. More money doesn't mean less poverty. In fact, there are some people that are poorer on $40,000 and $45,000 a year than others that are doing fine on $20,000 and $25,000 a year or even less.

POVERTY IS A RESULT OF CHOICES

It is not the size of your income that decides your level of poverty, contrary to what our government would tell us. There will always be poor people because there are causes for poverty that cannot be totally removed. In fact, many people choose poverty. Most of them don't choose poverty by saying they want to be poor, but they choose what causes their poverty. Poverty will never be fully solved this side of the millennium. It may still be around during the millennium because there will be some people with a sinful nature, and that is all it takes to have poverty.

CHAPTER 1: CAUSES AND CURES OF POVERTY

God's laws on finance are not likely going to get written up in the Wall Street Journal because the world does not think like God does. Notice **Proverbs 30:8, 9**,

> *"Remove far from me vanity and lies: give me neither poverty nor riches; feed me with food convenient for me: Lest I be full, and deny thee, and say, "Who is the LORD? or lest I be poor, and steal, and take the name of my God in vain."*

Have you ever heard of asking the Lord not to make you rich? This Scripture is saying that the writer wants to live on a level somewhere between poverty and riches. Do you think that we could get the Wall Street Journal or even most of the religious journals to do an article on that prayer?

Also in this passage, we see that wealth has problems as does poverty. This man is so poor that his stomach is wrapped around his backbone and he is not sure if he can eat a full piece of bread. He is so desperate that he steals to keep from collapsing dead from hunger. He is saying, "Lord save me from poverty so that I don't steal, so that I don't compromise to earn my living, and so I won't speak in a way that I shouldn't." But then he is also saying, "Lord, please don't let me get riches."

The Apostle Paul said that he had learned,

> *"...in whatsoever state I am, therewith to be content. I know both how to be abased, and I know how to abound: everywhere and in all things I am instructed both to be full and to be hungry"* **(Philippians 4:11).**

LEARNING TO BE CONTENT

There is the matter of learning to be content in whatever station of life God has placed you, rather than seeking poverty or wealth.

Let me remind you that in the passage in Proverbs it is Solomon speaking. Can you imagine that? If you read Ecclesiastes, he will tell you that riches don't have the answer. Here he fears becoming so rich that he might feel he would not need God's help. That is exactly why some people want to get rich – so that they won't have to trust God for anything. They don't want to pray. *"Give us this day our daily bread."* They don't even want to ask the Lord to give them their yearly bonus. They want to quit working like God said was healthy and right for us to do, and live the life of a loafer. We need to need God. Solomon is asking the Lord to save him from these two extremes. There are problems with both of them.

THE SIGNIFICANCE OF INCOME AMOUNTS

Keep in mind also that some Christians can prosper on less than what amounts to poverty to others. The amount of your income determines only to a degree how you live. This thought can be carried to an extreme by saying that you can't live like you are making $50,000 when you are really only bringing home $15,000. Still some people can live like they only have $15,000 coming in when they actually have $50,000. There is much more to poverty than the actual dollar level of income.

How many people do you know that have said that if they got a better job they would be better off? Then they got the better job and fell deeper into debt. They thought that riches would be the answer but they didn't know how to handle the riches. It is amazing how some people will drop in their income, and find out that less went further than more. In fact, they recover themselves faster than when they were making more and winding up further in debt.

Frequently, the more money made, the deeper the debt level, and the less made, the less debt. Your banker feels the same way – the less you make, the less he will let you go in debt and the more you make, the more he wants you to go in debt. They don't want to loan money to those that "need" it because they want to make sure they get it back – from those that didn't "need" it. That is how lending institutions think, and if you have money in the bank, that is how you want them to think. You don't want them loaning money to people that can't pay it back, because in such cases you might not get your money back and the bank would go under.

SCRIPTURE ASKS US TO CONSIDER THE CAUSE OF THE POOR

Let us look at the Scripture which will be our key text,

> *"The righteous considereth the cause of the poor: but the wicked regardeth not to know it."* **(Proverbs 29:7)**

God says that if you are righteous you are going to want to know why people are poor and what the causes are. It is amazing the practical truths of God's Word. When God saved us, He not only made us positionally righteous, but practically righteous also, and told us to stay in a righteous condition. He wants us to live that way and one of the marks of the righteous is that they consider the cause of the poor.

The problem is we have been trying to solve poverty without knowing the cause. The righteous person is going to seek, search, find out, figure, and learn. They are going to consider what caused the poverty and therefore will know something about how to cure poverty – in themselves or in others.

A VICIOUS CYCLE

Many Christians have come to me saying they were in a financial mess. Seldom did they know exactly how they got there, but they wanted to get out. I urge them to find out how they fell in, because no one gets out of such a mess until he first finds out how he got there. The alternative to this is that if you remove a person from their poverty, you have only to allow them time and they will be right back into it. Unless they can find the cause, they won't know the cure. The doctor who only deals with symptoms instead of causes never sees his patients get well.

We must soberly consider the cause as to why we are all poorer than we need to be, paying attention to all the aspects. You may not have a problem in one given area, but in years to come you may be able to help someone else out of that very trap. I have found that helping young couples in this realm has opened them up to the gospel. They found that I cared more about them than whether I was getting a decision that I could record in a booklet. The one thing that is about as close to a person's heart as anything is his financial condition. If you learn to help someone, he might be willing to listen to the God of your help.

THE BIBLE HAS A FINANCIAL PHILOSOPHY

The Bible has a financial philosophy that the world knows nothing about. Two or three generations ago, the world was operating by a Biblical philosophy because our godly forefathers had preached these things. They quit preaching it, and now the church has accepted a "foreign" philosophy financially. If we can get back to the Biblical way, we can offer financial sanity to an insane world.

Things may be going fairly well with the economy now, but in our lifetime, we will go through another recession or depression somewhere down the road. It won't hurt to get ready ahead of time. When Christians regarded financial issues rightly during the bad times, they had measures of revival. But it hasn't happened the last several times around. This may be partly because we have lost a Biblical philosophy in this area. We got into the same turmoil and the same thinking as the world, and thus we had nothing to offer.

There is a teaching today that I am opposed to. It is that it is the pastor's job to catch the "gold" fish. By this, it is meant that everyone is to go out and reach people, but the pastor's responsibility is to spend his time reaching the wealthy people in the community so they can bank-roll the church program. He selects certain people to reach and spends his time with them because they have money. I don't find anything like that in the Scriptures. One of the marks of Jesus' life is that He was preaching the gospel to the poor. The Bible doesn't tell us that He selected the rich so that He could get the church started off right financially. But I would remind you that with the preaching of the gospel to the poor, there were some that weren't as poor – not spiritually but financially.

POOR PEOPLE DON'T JUST HAPPEN

Poor people don't just happen. There is a reason for it. If there is a cause why someone is poor, until there is a cure found they will stay poor. If a town had a water tower that they couldn't keep water in, they might be able to remedy that if they found the reason for it – a hole in the tower. They may say that it just happened that way, but it will keep happening that way if they don't fix it. Oftentimes our purses are full of holes. We need to find out why they are full of holes, what the holes are, how they are formed and plug them up if we are going to be able to handle what we have and handle it correctly. The point here is that some people are living poorer on more because they have holes in their purses.

GOD'S RULES WORK

Not all of these causes are going to make sense to the mind of a lost person, but I remind you that this is the inspired Word of God. He is revealing the economics of heaven and the economics of earth. These verses were not written to fit into a capitalistic society under democratic or republican type government. I am not referring to parties but rather, styles of government. These verses were written under a different economy and different government, different nationality and another part of the world. Still, they are God's rules and they will work under any government and economy because the Word of God is not bound by the philosophies of man. This will not only work in America, but in Russia, China, Africa, etc.

As to the causes of poverty, some of them are found in the lives of everyone, to some degree or another. Most of us could do better with what we have if we would just learn some laws of God. It is dangerous to violate His laws in the handling of the material realm of life. Over the years, God has greatly helped me in some of these areas. I have had to put them into practice and sometimes learn the lessons the hard way before God would let me speak on them.

A young couple, learning these lessons at the outset of their marriage, could save themselves and profit from it upwards to tens of thousands of dollars in the course of their time together. I expect most of us could profit thousands of dollars. The average American income is now running over a million dollars in a lifetime. (If a person earned $33,000 a year, in thirty years he would have earned a million.) The average American family is making an excess of $25,000 a year and in forty years they will have handled over a million dollars. You may not be making $25,000 – but if you will learn from these lessons, how to save and invest some, you will be able to make $12,000 up to $15,000 from investments and working on the side.

We used to think that a million dollars was only for the rich, but a million is for the average in America today. What kind of an accounting are we going to make for those million dollars that we handled in our sojourn here on earth? God may teach you enough on this that you might make a million-and-a-half before it's all over. Poverty is not tied to the amount of money that passes through our hands – it is how much sticks, and how much we lost.

I remind you that when God made everything, He said that it was good. He planted a garden and set man to work. He was able to take care of the birds, lilies, the plants and animals of the fields. He is certainly able to take care of His people. God has laid down Biblical laws and principles to teach us how to operate here on earth. These are often abused. Let's begin looking at some of the causes of poverty and then what the cure is.

CHAPTER 2

DOING BUSINESS WITH GREEDY PEOPLE

Proverbs 1:17-19 says,

> *"Surely in vain the net is spread in the sight of any bird. And they lay wait for their own blood; they lurk privily for their own lives. So are the ways of every one that is greedy of gain; which taketh away the life of the owners thereof."*

When a bird sees you spreading a net out for him, he has sense enough to stay away.

The sad thing is that many humans don't have the sense of a bird when it comes to people that are greedy. Most of us know some greedy people who are out to get all that they can. If birds know enough to stay away from nets that they can see – what should you do as far as doing business with someone that is greedy?

If I told you about a used car dealer somewhere nearby that planned to rip off everyone that bought a car from him, would you be willing to come and ask me where that car lot was so that you could stay away from it? What do you know about the moral integrity and motivation of most of the people with whom you do business? One reason that some people are poor is that they don't bother to check out whether a person they are doing business with is greedy or not. I know from talking with a life insurance salesman years ago that many times they are pressured to sell policies that bring in quantities of money for the company but don't give much in benefits to the customer. Wouldn't you like to know whether your agent is honest or greedy when he suggests certain policies to you?

A person that doesn't pay attention to this rule is going to get "taken." They tend to think that they are so smart they can outsmart a greedy businessman who has just been waiting for someone like them to come along.

An honest person may charge you a little more, but you actually come out ahead in the end. Shoddy workmanship is often the evidence of a greedy heart. They may have the lowest price but do the poorest job. In fact, it may cost you more to make up for what they did, than what you saved by getting the cheapest item or service.

WHAT IS THE CURE?

The cure when dealing with greedy people is simple – don't! Find those that you can trust and deal with them. It used to be that success in business was tied to a good name. Now it is tied to the fast sell. Years ago, people used to want to make sure that businessmen had a right heart in their business. We would be wise to heed their example.

CHAPTER 3

SLEEPING TOO MUCH

Proverbs 6:10-11 says,

> *"Yet a little sleep, a little slumber, a little folding of the hands to sleep: So shall they poverty come as one that travelleth, and thy want as an armed man."*

The fatal flaw here is sleeping too much. Everyone needs to sleep and different people need different amounts of sleep. Different kinds of work and health conditions can affect this. However, if you get too much sleep you will be just as tired as if you didn't get enough, and that will make you want to sleep even more.

The Devil is not stupid. If you require eight hours sleep and he can get you to take 10 then you will think you need 12. And if you could earn 50¢ an hour just by working for yourself, that is $2 a day that he stole from you. That makes over $700 a year. In ten years, you would have $7,000 in the bank, plus interest. That constant sleeping not only robs us of our opportunities, but also robs us of our energy. I am not saying to cut your sleep too short so that you are sick, but there is such a thing as sleeping too much. A student in school that is always sleeping doesn't do well. A person on a job that is always sleeping doesn't do well either.

Proverbs 20:13 says,

> *"Love not sleep, lest thou come to poverty; open thine eyes, and thou shalt be satisfied with bread."*

Some people love sleep as much as any person that has season tickets to see their favorite baseball team. Every chance they get, they sleep. For some, it is an escape mechanism to get away from reality, hoping maybe they can dream or at least shut out their problems. Having that attitude towards sleep will make you poor. Recognize sleep as a necessity and not as something to be loved. Enjoy it only in the sense that it makes it possible for you to get on with what you want and need to do. Keep in mind that you will spend a third of your life asleep if you only get a normal amount of sleep. A person that lives until 60 years of age will spend 40 years awake and 20 years asleep. If he sleeps too much he may not even get 40 years awake.

"Open thou mine eyes,…" **(Psalm 119:18).**

Did you know that your eyes don't open naturally when you wake up? I realize some of you may have never experienced this, but others of us wake up in the morning not even sure we want to look to see if the sun is up. There are times that with conscious effort we need to obey God and open our eyes.

Another verse on this subject is found in **Proverbs 23:21**,

> *"For the drunkard and the glutton shall come to poverty: and drowsiness shall clothe a man with rags."*

A drowsy spirit when you are awake and sort of fumbling through life can make a man poor.

WHAT IS THE CURE? Don't get too much sleep. If you don't have this problem, just remember it for someone who does.

CHAPTER 4

TRAVELING

Proverbs 6:11 says,

> *"So shall thy poverty come as one that travelleth, and thy want as an armed man."*

Traveling can cause poverty.

I remember a professor in college who had figured out that if he bought a house within walking distance of the college, he could pay thousands of dollars more for the house. That would still allow him to put money in the bank every year besides, because it meant he had one less vehicle to buy, keep up, insure, etc. He wouldn't have to join a health club because he would get his exercise walking back and forth. He had a savings of time because of the amount of time he saved going back and forth to the college. He was able to make money, save it, and invest it while some of the others were having it hard. He realized the high expense of traveling back when gas was less than a quarter a gallon and you could buy a new Volkswagen for just over $2,000.

Can you imagine what the cost of traveling is now? You can evaluate a person on their gross income, but if there is much traveling involved in his job, you have not touched what he must have to live on. Consider some of the expenses of traveling: the amount of time it takes, the amount of energy it uses, the amount of expense for making these trips, and the division of your efforts between where you live and where you are working.

Some people travel and travel and travel, never realizing this is causing, to some degree, their financial distress. A person either must have a good amount of money, be willing to be poor, be able to produce a large income from the travel, or else set strict limits on the travel. It may be necessary to travel, but even then, we better count the cost. We as Americans think it is just our right to be able to travel. It may be your right, but it could be your undoing financially. I am not saying don't travel, but just take into consideration the cost.

WHAT IS THE CURE?

Count the cost of traveling and evaluate what it is doing for you financially. There may need to be some adjustments made.

CHAPTER 5

LOOSE MORAL LIVING

Proverbs 6:26 says,

> *"For by means of a whorish woman a man is brought to a piece of bread: and the adulteress will hunt for the precious life."*

Loose living morally is financially expensive. I know there is a price to be paid because of the sin – the effects on the body, the loss of reputation, the loss of self-image, and a loss of time and energy. But there is a financial loss also. A person getting into this is going to lose. There is no way that they are going to win. It costs and costs and costs.

This verse was written before our day, for now there is child support required for the children that are born out of wedlock. I have listened to men ask me how it is that they are paying for something that they did years ago. They complain, "It comes out of my paycheck every week, and the court decides how much to take out!" I remind them that they broke God's law and that costs. No one had ever told them.

God says that it will cost financially to live immorally. There is an awesome price tag on this area of sin! Some sins don't seem to have that kind of penalty, but have other consequences. With this sin a man can be brought down to just a piece of bread and be made glad to have a piece of bread. You may say that it isn't that bad in America, but I could give you names of people that would show you that it is bad. I know of some people scared to death to get a raise for fear that all of the raise and a little more will be taken from them by the court to support children for which they are legally responsible. If fact, some of them are ready to quit their jobs because they are better off on welfare than when they have to pay child support, all because they had gotten involved with a whorish woman back in their younger days. While they were "sowing their wild oats", they thought little of the harvest it would bring in their life. If a person had a great sense in this area, he would know to stay out of it, even if the only concern was for his wallet.

Sometimes blackmail comes to a person who has been successful financially. Someone may try to blackmail their marriage, etc. If a man were living loosely with a whorish woman 15 or 20 years ago, then later decided to run for city council, don't you think an unprincipled person can collect a good bit of money just to keep quiet? You may wonder why someone makes good money and doesn't have anything. It is because they have violated God's laws of poverty.

Another passage on this same subject is found in **Proverbs 5:3-8**,

> *"For the lips of a strange woman drop as an honeycomb, and her mouth is smoother than oil: But her end is bitter as wormwood, sharp as a twoedged sword. Her feet go down to death; her steps take hold on hell. Lest thou shouldest ponder the path of life, her ways are moveable, and thou canst not know them. Hear me now therefore, O ye children, and depart not from the words of my mouth. Remove thy way far from her, and come not nigh the door of her house:"*

In verse 3, it says she is a sweet talker – like a honeycomb. Some of you know this to be true by experience and that the next verse can be read in your life. What started out one way, ended so differently. Verses 9 and 10 from the same chapter go on to say, Lest thou give thine honour unto others, and thy years unto the cruel: Lest strangers be filled with thy wealth; and thy labours be in the house of a stranger;" You will end up working for somebody else.

We live in such a wretched Sodom and Gomorrah that it has gone beyond boys with girls to boys with boys and girls with girls. There is money that moves in those realms, but nothing of honest industry goes on. There is no benefit, product, or service that is Biblically honorable that is produced here. Whenever money moves in something that is not a right industry, service, or product, it becomes wasted money. An Olympic gold medalist diver has a tarnished image because of his sodomy. His name is known better for his immorality than for his accomplishments.

The person who lives immorally finds that he is pouring his money and efforts into someone else's pockets. He may not have intended it to be that way, but God said that it would be even if He has to route the money this way or that. You may say that there will be no money exchanged, but God will get the money down the road moved into other pockets. There are some people that well after the time of their looseness morally are paying the price that God's Word said would be paid. Loose morals cost, and they cause poverty. The more we tolerate it in America, the poorer we are going to be.

WHAT IS THE CURE?

The cure for this cause of poverty is to stay away from loose living and loose morals, and those that get involved therein. This is not to say that you are not to witness to them, but don't in any sense compromise yourself or be drawn that direction in any way. There is a handicap put on a person going that route.

CHAPTER 6

LIVING WICKEDLY

Proverbs 10:2-3 says,

> *"Treasures of wickedness profit nothing: but righteousness delivereth from death. The LORD will not suffer the soul of the righteous to famish: but He casteth away the substance of the wicked."*

The fifth cause is simply this – living wickedly. Violating the laws of God will eventually lead a nation, an area, a family, or an individual to poverty. God said that He would "cast away the substance of the wicked."

Picture this: The lost person doesn't know God, and won't even believe this picture unless he has seen the final result of it. A wicked man is piling up his money, but what he doesn't see is that God is on the other side of the pile grabbing it and casting it away. Though the man has piled it up, he can't figure why the pile doesn't grow as fast as he thinks it ought to. In fact, the more he puts on, the less he ends up with.

I have read the biographies of wealthy families that went broke because of living wickedly. They gathered large sums of money – not just $100,000 or a million – but more like $100 million and $500 million. Some built cathedral-like churches and then donated them to the Roman Catholic church, but within a generation they were absolutely broke. I have kept some of these biographies, because a lost person was writing about lost people and how they got and lost their wealth, never realizing that they were giving me illustrations of what God's Word had taught all along. A person that chooses to live wickedly is begging God to take what they have away, and sooner or later, He will do it. We are reviewing the laws of how God operates whether the economy agrees with it or not. There are many people suffering poverty and loss of finances because the *"treasures of wickedness profit nothing."* Don't you feel sorry for those people who live wickedly?

Does anyone know who the relatives of those Pharaohs or the Caesars were? They were the wealthiest men in their day. No one kept track of that just as no one has any idea who is related to Nebuchadnezzar. What about those that struck it rich in the gold mines while they lived wickedly out in the West? Have you ever read stories of those people – wealthy one day and poor the next? They couldn't seem to figure out what happened. God's Word has been explaining their problem all along.

A government that will encourage wickedness and try to solve poverty at the same time, you can be sure, will fail in solving poverty. The removing of wickedness is an economic blessing to a nation because one of the causes of poverty is erased.

WHAT IS THE CURE?

The cure is very simple – get rid of the wickedness. Look at what the previous verses say about the righteous. Verse 3 says,

> *"The LORD will not suffer the soul of the righteous to famish:"*

God said in verse 2,

> *"...but righteousness delivereth from death".*

David said in **Psalm 37:25** that he had

> *"not seen the righteous forsaken, nor his seed begging bread."*

CHAPTER 6: LIVING WICKEDLY

Proverbs 11:4 says,

> *"Riches profit not in the day of wrath: but righteousness delivereth from death."*

Righteousness is the cure for this cause of poverty.

CHAPTER 7

DEALING WITH A SLACK HAND

Proverbs 10:4 says,

> *"He becometh poor that dealeth with a slack hand: but the hand of the diligent maketh rich."*

Someone who operates without any concern about what happens to their money is going to be poor. Easy come, easy go – spending it like water – they don't really keep track of their money. The cure is given in the verse – *"the hand of the diligent maketh rich."* It doesn't say anything about environment, opportunity, government, skills, health, strength or age. Diligence and a slack hand are set in contrast. One will make for wealth and the other for poverty.

I am not concerned about getting wealthy as far as the world looks at it, but about having finances available as the needs arise. Contrast this with being so far behind on things that a person wonders if he is even going to survive. That is how the poor operate.

WHAT IS THE CURE?

Be diligent. Let me give you several suggestions on the cure for this cause and what it means to be diligent. I believe that a person needs to be cautious when they handle their money. It is not wastepaper. You don't just throw it around. It represents time and opportunity. Do you have a budget of some sort? Do you have an idea of what you need to spend and how you need to spend it? It is amazing how people got along on so little during the Depression. But if you will crawl up in the attic, you will find that they kept track of every penny that they spent. The ones that didn't do that don't have an attic for you to crawl into.

I am not talking about necessarily enslaving yourself to a piece of paper, but there ought to be some idea of what one needs this week, next week, next month, and the rest of the year, etc. This will let you know if your income is going to match your outgo, or whether you need to do some praying, or get some extra work. God may miraculously deliver, but so often we tempt God in the realm of finances.

What do I mean "tempt" God? Don't the Scriptures teach that God would have the angels keep charge over Jesus and that they would bear Him up if He so much as stumbled? Satan reminded Jesus of that when he had Him on the pinnacle of the temple. Satan told Jesus that He could throw Himself down from there and that the angels would take care of Him because that's what the Scriptures promised. Jesus said,

> *"Thou shalt not tempt the Lord thy God"* **(Matthew 4:7)**.

The meaning of this – you take care of what you can take care of and the promises are there for what you aren't able to care for. Many people won't take care of what they can, and they still expect God to supply for them. That is called tempting God. There are people that are always trying to force God into a corner to deliver them. God told us to learn to be diligent. If you keep dealing with that slack hand, He may just tell the angel to go ahead and let you fall and learn a lesson. You can read in the Old and New Testaments about what happened to those that tempted God. Acts 5 tells what happened to Ananias and Sapphira when they tempted God.

Not only should you keep track of what you are going to spend in the future, keep track of what you spent in the past. If

CHAPTER 7: DEALING WITH A SLACK HAND

you know where it went you will know whether to be happy or sad about it, and what you can do in the future to change things. A lot of people don't like checkbooks because it tells how much they spent here and there. They would like to think that it was just a few dollars, when in reality, it was much more, and more often than they want to face.

Learn to be accountable. After all, we are going to have to give an account to God and the records will be there. We are also going to give account of ourselves and our stewardship. It was a continuing theme throughout Jesus' parables – we are going to have to give an account of what we have committed to us in the material realm. Some of us are going to have bigger accounts to give than others because we had more committed to us.

Examining how I have dealt in the past will help me in the future. Are we going to be slack about the past and continue to be slack in the future? Such will make us poor. Or are we going to be diligent about the past and the future, and diligent about what is put in our hands so that we will have more of it left?

There ought to be definite goals. What do you plan to accomplish financially? Do you have any financial goals as to how much debt you want paid off by the end of the year? How much saving would you like to have set aside? Where do you want to be financially by the end of the year? Or, do you think what happens will happen? Can you imagine a farmer looking out at this fields and saying that he has had good crops other years and he's not sure whether he will have corn or soy beans out in that field but whatever will be will be, and he will just see how it turns out? He will have a lot of weeds! A person must make some plans! This is true in all areas of our life. This is part of being diligent.

After you have established goals, diligently and honestly

consider what is possible and what is necessary to pray about. What are your plans for reaching those goals? The difference between a goal and a dream is that you must have a plan for reaching your goals. Your dreams are just sort of hoping you might reach them somehow.

When you start to lay plans, you may find that some things that you thought were goals were just dreams that you had. Unless God does something supernaturally along the way, you will never obtain them. God might graciously operate, but it is amazing how often He blesses those that are diligent and how often He strips those that are wicked. Didn't He make things prosper in the hands of Joseph and Daniel? God can do that. The diligent are those that He will prosper. Why should He prosper those with a slack hand if they are going to waste a good percentage of it anyway?

A few years from now, if Jesus tarries His coming, you might be able to give more to missions and the church and be able to help in certain other areas than if you had continued to deal with a slack hand. The Devil delights in Christians being loose with their money, and letting it slither through their fingers. I am convinced that God entrusts enough wealth to His people to take care of all the missionaries that He ever sends, but the missionaries are having to do without because some of those that were entrusted with it haven't taken proper care of it.

Have some sort of budget. Be cautious with your money. Be diligent about how you handle it. Have accountability for the past, a goal for the future, and a plan for how you are going to achieve it. This is a cure that won't solve everything by midnight tonight, but you might be a whole lot better off by December 31st if you start with it now.

CHAPTER 8

LACK OF DEFENSE OR PROTECTION

Proverbs 10:15 says,

> *"The rich man's wealth is his strong city: the destruction of the poor is their poverty."*

The first few times I read this verse, I thought it was one we couldn't do much about, but I kept reading and became convinced that there was something that could be done. *"The rich man's wealth is his strong city..."* In those days, they built walls around their cities. Some of them didn't bother because they figured everything would keep going like it had been, and that there would always be a time of peace and prosperity. You may say that it costs to build a defense, but a good defense pays and doesn't cost.

I know that there are many holes in our national defense budget, but I am thankful that it has been a long time since any nation dared to try to invade America. I have been in countries that have been invaded time and time again. These countries have beautiful geography, hard-working people, natural resources – but are still poor because anyone that wants to can come and run over them, taking what they have. We need to realize that wicked people are going to be around until Jesus comes and puts them in their place, and wicked people don't understand kindness. If you doubt that – volunteer to spend one week at the State penitentiary trying to be sweet, loving, and helpful to all the "residents". See if you can survive the week before you go to the hospital. I want you to know, there are some people who believe destruction is a way of living. Taking advantage of others is what they are going to do. If there is not law, protection, or defense they are going to get whatever they want.

Years ago, when I was visiting Dominica there was a bit of political unrest. On a certain night, I walked by a rally that was going on with an opponent to the ruling party that had been smuggled onto the island. He was up on the balcony of the second floor hollering and saying that all the guns had been taken off the island (it was illegal for anyone to own a gun), even for the militia. He was saying they were helpless and their neighbors could come and take them over. I'm not sure why he was so worried about their neighbors, when at the time we were paying 30¢ a pound for bananas in the States, and they were paying the people that grew them, and loaded them on the ships 3¢ a pound. Because they didn't have any way to protect themselves, anyone could do anything that they wanted and they didn't stand a chance. No national defense meant that anyone could take advantage economically.

They tell me that a farmer makes 2¢ or 3¢ for the wheat in a loaf of bread. You have to wonder if someone doesn't need some protection economically, even in the United States.

WHAT IS THE CURE?

There needs to be some protection. The ravages of war cause poverty. Some of you may have been to Vietnam and have seen what happened there. Others of us may have seen pictures. If you have ever seen anything like that you will appreciate a defense that keeps people from wanting to come in and walk all over us. One of the reasons that our country is so rich is not that we are so great, but that we have protected ourselves.

CHAPTER 9

STINGINESS IN GIVING

Proverbs 11:24 reads,

> *"There is that scattereth, and yet increaseth; and there is that withholdeth more than is meet, but it tendeth to poverty."*

Look at this verse in the light of stinginess in giving.

Let me illustrate by using gardens and farms. There is an old expression used during times of famine. "Don't eat your seed corn." You need it if you are not going to starve the next year so you can scatter it to get an increase. But if you decide that you are hungry enough that you want to eat it now, or you are going to hold onto it rather than scatter it, that will lead to poverty.

There is a Biblical principle in Malachi when he asks, "Will a man rob God?" We see a principle in II Corinthians 9 about reaping what we sow. If we sow sparingly, we will also reap sparingly, and if we sow bountifully, we will reap bountifully. That passage is referring to giving. A person doesn't really give to a church. Hopefully they give to God, and God will not allow anyone to out give Him.

Really, you are investing with God. You are planting seed – a little or a lot, depending on what kind of a harvest you want down the road – a little one or a large one or perhaps no harvest at all. A person that decides to withhold more than is meet is stingy and literally saying to God, "I can do better without your blessings than I can with them. I have had so many of your blessings that I would like a rest for a while, and am going to take a sabbatical. I'm not going to plant anything with you. Then when things get tight again I will start giving." They don't realize that is what they are really saying.

It is like the fellow that worked for a company where every man signed up for an insurance policy except this man. He didn't want them taking a little bit out of his check. The agreement was that everyone had to sign or no one got the benefits. After his fellow workers realized he wasn't going to do it, they jumped him and were about to kill him. He told them to wait just a minute and went back to tell the boss he had decided he did want that policy – his co-workers had explained it a little differently than his boss had. Sometimes God must come along with a big stick and explain things to us in a way that we have never thought of before. God says, "There is that scattereth yet increaseth..." He tells us in His Word and if we don't heed it, He chastens us in the area of our finances.

WHAT IS THE CURE?

The cure is obviously Biblical – be open-hearted, be generous, be intelligent by knowing where it is going, be right in the matter of your giving and realize that it is an investment for the future. It is a guaranteed investment to come back in multiples (if not in this life - in the next one). We are laying up treasures over on the other side. Some people think that they can't afford to give, but what they are really saying is that they can't afford to be blessed. You have to feel sorry for someone that doesn't understand the laws of planting and reaping, and the matter of giving and getting.

CHAPTER 10

WEALTH GOTTEN BY VANITY

Proverbs 13:11 says,

> *"Wealth gotten by vanity shall be diminished: but he that gathereth by labour shall increase."*

There is a right and wrong way to make money. How you make it often determines whether you get to hang on to some of it. God states and guarantees that if you get it by vanity it will decrease. Do you want your money to grow or shrink? Vanity will decrease it and labor will increase it.

Vanity has the idea of emptiness, something that is transitory or passing, or something that is unsatisfactory. The dictionary says that it means to be idle or worthless, futile, to operate on pride, self-satisfaction, or falsehood. Matthew Henry, commenting on the verse, said, "It is people that gain their wealth by feeding their pride or the pride of others, operating in the realm of luxury, getting their money by gaming or playing on the stage, by fraud of by lying." It is interesting what they said in the 1600's on this subject.

What does getting money by vanity mean? Some people obtain money by flattery. Some get it by pride or by building up other people's pride. Some do it based on the matter of appearances and how things look. These things are tied to vanity in the Bible. God says if you get it that way, it will shrink. Can you picture their pile of money just shrinking? If they get it wickedly, God is going to cast it away, or if they get it by vanity, He will just shrink it down.

By the way of contrast, here is a poor man slaving and

laboring to get his money. He has only a little, but God causes it to increase. The world cannot figure that out. You won't have to think long before you can remember someone who, by labor, saw something increase and those that by vanity saw it decrease. We must be concerned about how we earn our money. There are various con artists and shysters – perfectly legal – but operating on people's vanity or their own vanity and obtaining money that way. But they can't hang onto it. It is not the initial amount, but rather how much God lets you keep, that counts.

WHAT IS THE CURE?

The cure obviously is labor. If you look carefully at the verse it states, He that gathereth by labour shall increase." He has produced some good, some object, or some item. He may have improved some item through workmanship, such as taking a board and making a table from it. It may be that someone has been able to grow something or a service has been provided for people. A shepherd might not do much for his sheep except take care of them, but he does get a benefit for just taking care of sheep and watching over them. There is the realm of services as well as goods.

Let me share a story of personal testimony with you to further illustrate this point. As a boy, I grew up in a small town where there were some poor widows, and some were of poor health so that they couldn't shovel their sidewalks, mow their lawns, or clean up in the fall. I tried to help them, and they would give me what they could. I was laughed at for it, but I had been taught that it was better to labor than to sit. I also had learned that it was better to work for a nickel than to work for Dad – because I didn't get my nickel then! I also knew those widows didn't make me work as hard as Dad did. (Dad knew that and did it intentionally so that I would go out and work.)

CHAPTER 10: WEALTH GOTTEN BY VANITY

I wanted to go to college, but couldn't get any money together. I continued to labor on through my senior year and into the summer following. I was able to get enough money to apply to a nearby college and was accepted. People asked me if I was going to college and I would tell them, "Yes." When was I going? "This fall." Do you have your money for the first semester?" "No." "How are you going to pay your way?" "Don't know – I have just been praying and God has made it clear that somehow it is going to be cared for." "What are you doing to be able to care for it?" I hadn't been able to find much of anything as far as a job because it was a time of recession. "I am working, but I am not making much." People said that was foolish – better not to work they thought. I figured a little was better than nothing. Now today, I know that though that thought is a little out-dated, it is still Biblical.

A man paid me $15.00 to cut down a tree and cut it up into firewood. It was all caught up in the electrical lines and I would go up and cut one branch out at a time. He had to pay me $5.00 a month for three months just to cover my pay. I was afraid that he was going to have trouble getting his groceries. I did it because I felt I needed to try to help him. I sold newspapers as well. One of the men to whom I sold newspapers said that he would like to have his house painted and wondered if I could do it. I offered to paint it for an amount that would have made anyone who painted for a living angry with me. I worked hard painting that house, thinking that if I did a good job I might be able to find another house to paint before school started. I was painting one Saturday when he asked me to help him put up some dry wall on the ceiling of a room that he was fixing for his wife. Now, he wasn't paying me to do that – he was just paying me to paint the house. You know how some people add to contracts, but I went to help anyway.

He told me he would set it up and I could just nail it in there.

I responded that I thought it would be better if I held it and he nailed it. He said that he was trying to give me the easier job. To this I answered, I was taking the easier one. I told him that my problem was that I was blind in one eye and I didn't always hit the nail every time I swung the hammer. With dry wall that is not such a good idea. He asked me if I had graduated from high school, and did I have a scholarship to go to college? He added that I could get a scholarship for being blind in one eye. Now, I had heard of many scholarships, but never that one. He went on to say that he was coming home from work one day and there was a fellow in the rain. He had picked him up and the man had given him a card, saying that he was trying to help people that were handicapped. He found the card in his pocket and said for me to call this fellow and tell him that I was blind in one eye. Perhaps he could help me with college.

I thought that was better than painting houses! I checked into it and got help financially for four years of college due to being blind in one eye. This resulted from helping someone put up dry wall, for which I was not getting paid! I got the job painting the house because I had been helping some widows. Don't try to tell me that labor doesn't pay off, and God can't increase what a man gets by laboring.

Shortly after that, a man who was a manager of a large shoe store had been observing me and asked my dad what kind of work I was going to get through college. When my dad told him that I didn't have a job yet, he said that he needed someone that knew how to work. When he offered me a job, I gratefully took it. When that job closed there was a hardware store that wanted me because they had seen me working around the town. The point I am making is this – God can increase what a person gets by laboring. If I had chosen to be lazy, or to wait for a good paying job I might never have gotten started in college, and may never have gotten through.

CHAPTER 10: WEALTH GOTTEN BY VANITY

God's laws work whether they are understood or not. I am giving testimony to this principle. What happened to me has happened to so many other people and it is not glory to a person, but rather glory to God Who keeps His laws in operation.

CHAPTER 11

REFUSING INSTRUCTION

Proverbs 13:18 says,

> "Poverty and shame shall be to him that refuseth instruction: but he that regardeth reproof shall be honoured."

Verse 8 of the same chapter says,

> "The ransom of a man's life are his riches: but the poor heareth not rebuke."

One of the causes of poverty and marks of a poor person who will remain poor, is that he doesn't hear any instruction, won't take any advice, and won't be corrected on how he handles things. He has a know-it-all attitude. He is always telling others, but never listening for himself. You can talk until you are blue in the face, but he is not interested in any correction, advice, or instruction. Some will only listen as a means to get your money.

I have talked to a few rich people and it is amazing how little they claim to know. Further, I have talked to some poor people and it is amazing how they have the answers to everything. Go where people are totally broke and begging, and they will tell you how to do most any kind of job. They have an answer for any problem in the government, and they have a solution for all the things that are going on around them. On the other hand, someone who has a little bit of this world's goods isn't so sure on everything. He doesn't have all the answers and may even ask your advice on something! Such people are always searching for help and looking for some input. Still others are poor because they are trying to figure out all the answers instead of doing anything.

WHAT IS THE CURE?

The cure is found in **Proverbs 13:18**,

"He that regardeth reproof shall be honoured."

The cure is to hear other people. Listen to them and let it linger in your mind. Think back over it – the examples, the correction, the instruction, and reproof you have had. Instead of defending yourself when someone says that you are going about a matter in a wrong way, find out what they are talking about. They may be right. The very fact that they said you were handling it wrong either means that they are one of the ignorant poor that is always babbling, or they cared enough for you to risk your friendship in trying to help you. Someone willing to risk a friendship is someone that really cares about you and will be able to give you some help and direction.

A person that values reproof will be honored by God. Hear it, hang on to it, think about it, remember it, sort out the advice, consider it and regard it in your mind. Follow the instruction that is good.

Proverbs 11:14 says,

"... in the multitude of counsellors there is safety."

Get masses of advice and you will learn to recognize that which is useless. Search it out from the Scriptures. Learn to follow good instruction. It may be your deliverance.

Many poor people say they are in such bad shape that there is no hope. I am amazed that the ones that think they are in the worst shape are not really so. I have sat down with some and shook my head and seen that it would take them five or six years to get straightened out, and others maybe ten years. But then

CHAPTER 11: REFUSING INSTRUCTION

there were some that thought there was no hope and that they would continue going deeper and deeper in debt. In two years, we could have had them out of all debt, but now it would take four years. They knew too much and now they are in worse shape. You can only help those that want help. Some people delight in a false humility, saying that they can't get out of debt. I don't believe that it has to be that way. I believe that the child of God can come to a place of obedience and pay back what they owe. They can reach a place where they are not bound up financially and better able to be used by God.

CHAPTER 12

TALK OF THE LIPS – NO LABOR

Proverbs 14:23 says,

> "In all labour there is profit: but the talk of the lips tendeth only to penury."

Many people don't believe the first part of this verse, but then, many people simply don't believe their Bibles. Penury means poverty – all you have is a couple of pennies to rub together instead of a couple of dollars.

Today, some have the idea that talking will make more money than working. The world will try to sell us on this kind of philosophy. The realm of sales is where people tend to think that talking makes the money. I have never known a successful salesman who made it by merely talking. Beneath the talk there had to be sweat, toil, experience, and effort. I have seen numerous failures that came and went, thinking they were going to talk themselves into riches instead of working

Let me use an example of a man that is somewhat successful in sales. For years, this man has been trying to encourage some people to sell sewing machines to the Amish out in the Midwest. He has found a number of folks who have been willing to try to talk people into buying them, but none of them have done very well or made very much. They don't understand that before this man sells a machine he goes over it piece by piece. He wants to know how that machine is put together, how it works, how it is to be repaired and adjusted. He has been able to sell a machine in a different color to someone who has just bought that same machine in the first color – because his machine worked and the other one did not. He had labored to have the machine timed and operating properly. This man can sell it for more than the person that took it out of the box that came from the factory, never checking to find it skips stitches if it stitches at all.

The point I am making is this – if you as a salesperson don't work on your product, you are not going to be able to talk people into it. You must get acquainted with it, study it, and put effort into it. The Bible says that the talk of the lips tendeth only to one thing, and that is penury or poverty. Putting effort into knowing your product is a mark of distinction between success and failure in the realm of sales.

This principle applies to any other area where talking is involved. For example, many preachers think that if they can talk well they will make good preachers. Having a gift of gab doesn't make for preaching. It is the laboring before God, laboring in the study, and laboring in prayer that gives you something worthwhile to tell others.

There is no doubt in my mind that there are people with a far greater way with words than I have, but the Lord has seen fit to give me more ministry than they have because they trusted in their ability to speak – "talk of the lips". I knew that would never pull me through. My wife can tell you what it was like before I went into the ministry and the early days in particular. I was a master at getting both feet in my mouth at the same time. And then had trouble getting any words out around them.

WHAT IS THE CURE?

Labor. Work. If there is no toil, sweat or labor you will not value what you get. You won't gain much to be able to value, and what's more, others won't value you very much.

There is no value in simply talking. But *"... in all labor there is profit"* according to the Bible (**Proverbs 14:23**). You may say,

CHAPTER 12: TALK OF THE LIPS—NO LABOR

there are some jobs that are a lot of work yielding very little pay. That may be the immediate result. I remember working in a hardware store where I was the poorest paid employee in the store – perhaps because I was a Christian. Another fellow simply drove around in a truck delivering appliances and received more pay than I did. I was the one who had to stack the appliances on top of each other, pull them down, get them ready to go out, etc. I decided that in all labor there is profit – though I was stuck in the store while he was out riding around, stopping to get a Coke here or there with the fellow that was in charge of setting the machine up. I more than doubled what I made in savings since then, even allowing for inflation, because I learned many things in that store. I learned a lot about people, and about fixing things. I figured that if they weren't going to pay me, I would get it by learning new skills.

I worked in a shoe store making low wages, but I tried to learn how they did business and advertised. It has been of value to me ever since. Some of the others were cutting corners to make a little more without putting in the work. I am the one that is better off, because in all labor there is profit. God promises, whether the boss sees it or not, there will be profit for those that labor. Our responsibility is to labor and God will take care of the profit.

There was a farmer, the father of two sons, on his death bed. He had a good farm, but it had to be worked and the boys tended to want to enjoy themselves. So he left them with this message,

> "There is a great treasure on this farm, and it is within 18 inches of the surface of the ground."

That was all he would tell them, and he died. They set their plow deep and worked the soil. About 15 or 20 years later they began to understand that there was a great treasure in that farm if you worked the farm and the soil.

Many people are trying to find the easy way to success and riches and trying to avoid the very thing that God blesses. There is a paymaster in Heaven that will balance accounts when people don't do right.

II Thessalonians 3:7-12 says,

> ***7** For yourselves know how ye ought to follow us: for we behaved not ourselves disorderly among you;* ***8*** *Neither did we eat any man's bread for nought; but wrought with labour and travail night and day, that we might not be chargeable to any of you:* ***9*** *Not because we have not power, but to make ourselves an ensample unto you to follow us.* ***10*** *For even when we were with you, this we commanded you, that if any would not work, neither should he eat.* ***11*** *For we hear that there are some which walk among you disorderly, working not at all, but are busybodies.* ***12*** *Now them that are such we command and exhort by our Lord Jesus Christ, that with quietness they work, and eat their own bread.*

Verse 10 is clear – those that will not work should not eat. *"In all labor there is profit"* – you get to eat!! God has ordained work for all mankind. Some can't produce as much as others, but God will see that there is profit that comes from all labor.

I have a friend from upstate New York who worked for the U.S Post Office and was in management there. His superiors came to him and told him they were in the process of a reorganization shuffle, they had a job for him, but needed to lay him off temporarily. They wanted him to collect unemployment because they were going to pay their share of it and felt it was owed him. They didn't want him to go out and try to get another job because

CHAPTER 12: TALK OF THE LIPS—NO LABOR

it would create a problem as far as their bringing him back in several weeks.

He went home that night and told his family that he had been laid off and that he would have work again in several weeks. The next morning he told his wife to pack him a lunch. They reminded him that he didn't have to go to work that day – but he told them that he did have to work that day – if he didn't, he wouldn't be able to eat supper that night because the Bible says, *"If any would not work, neither should he eat."* He got in his car and started down the road, going from farmer to farmer saying something like this:

> "I have been laid off from the Post Office and they insist that I take my unemployment. I will be going back to work in a matter of weeks. Do you have any work that I can do on your farm? I can't accept any pay, but I need to be able to face my wife and children tonight so that I can eat supper. Will you let me work on your farm for free?"

He finally found a farmer that would let him do that and he worked the whole time he was laid off. When it was time to go back to work he thanked the farmer and told him that he felt that he had earned his unemployment. The farmer began to understand that the laws of God need to be obeyed whether they make sense to the worldly mind or not. It gave him a testimony throughout the community that he couldn't have bought with money. God gave him some profit from that work, not just in groceries that came out of the farmer's garden, but eventually some lumber to build an addition onto his house. We need to realize our responsibility to labor.

CHAPTER 13

WASTEFULNESS

Proverbs 18:9 says,

> "He also that is slothful in his work is brother to him that is a great waster."

There are two causes found in this verse. 1. Wastefulness and 2. Slothfulness (see below).

The first one that I want to point out to you is:

A PERSON WHO IS WASTEFUL.

Wastefulness leads to poverty. Some of us have heard the saying, "Waste not, want not." This isn't Scripture, but is definitely Scriptural in principle. Many families in the world could survive out of the garbage cans of some Christians. We, in America, live in a throw-away society. Right now, they are designing cars that you throw away at 50,000 miles. Some of you thought you had one like that already! They can sell them to you cheaply and when they have gone so many miles nearly everything goes bad. Supposedly, it is cheap enough that you will be able to buy another one.

Think about how much of what we purchase gets thrown away. Just go into the poor parts of town and see the dumpsters they have for every several houses. Isn't that a lesson in a cause of poverty? Drive through town in the winter and notice the windows that are open because people are too lazy to turn a thermostat down. They will cool off by opening a window. They don't mind wasting the heat. You know who rents and who owns that way. Then they become upset if the landlord raises the rent.

We waste water, electricity, food and clothes. We wear them a little while and we don't like them so we throw them away or yard sale them. If a person had to put a garment together from the cotton originally, spin it into thread, weave the cloth, etc. they might decide to keep it a little longer no matter what happens to be the style. I am not saying that we need to look like we are broke, but there are myriads of people that are broke because of looking like they aren't.

There used to be a time that if a person bought anything from the Rescue Mission it was in order to make rugs, because that's how far gone the clothing was. But now you can find things there that make you wonder if they were ever worn. The clothes they have there are enough to rival most second-hand clothing stores. The newspaper recycling business is another example. We are so wasteful with what we have.

WHAT IS THE CURE?

We need to consider our lifestyle and values. Consider what it takes to satisfy us, and how long we will be satisfied. So often, we don't consider the long range. Look into the matter of recycling. Consider how leftovers will work into the next meal.

I knew a man that went to a Bible Institute and became the head cook in charge of ordering food. He ordered less food and the people ate better than they had ever eaten there before on much less money. You see, he figured out that what was leftover from one meal would fit into the menu later on, and they didn't have as much to throw away. He was able to figure out how much the people ate, and he didn't have an oversupply one meal and a shortage the next. He spent time studying and working it out.

It is a matter of frugality without becoming chintzy. There is a fine line here and we need to learn it so as not to be such wasteful people. Our money would last longer and go farther if

CHAPTER 13: WASTEFULNESS

we would consider the long run rather than the immediate. The answer is to have long-range goals and a plan of how to reach those goals. It might do us good to see how much food in the refrigerator spoils, goes in the garbage or down the disposal in a month. Then figure up how much that food was worth and what you could have done with that money. It just takes a little bit here and there to have a lot of money left over at the end of the year.

Let me give you a little phase that was given to me by Brother Bob Doom.

"Fix it up, wear it out, use it up, or do without."

You can become too tight, but it will deal with wastefulness. It is amazing how much we could do without, never really affecting our lifestyle, testimony, necessary needs, or comforts. I am not saying that we should become a "Scrooge" or that we should live bound up financially, but I think that if we can understand some principles we can stand back and evaluate where we are, where we are headed, and why. We might be able to get some things back in balance.

CHAPTER 14

SLOTHFULNESS

Proverbs 18:9 shows a second cause in the same verse,

> *"He also that is slothful in his work is brother to him that is a great waster."*

Slothfulness brings poverty as quickly as being wasteful. In fact, they are brothers to one another. What is slothfulness? I looked it up and found that it means to be lazy, to do as little as you can get by with, or to do it as late as possible, particularly when there are not reasons for it to be late. The slothful person is the one who was going to join the procrastinator's club, but just hasn't gotten around to it.

Let's look at what God says about the slothful person.

Proverbs 19:15 says,

> *"Slothfulness casteth into a deep sleep; and an idle soul shall suffer hunger."*

It is typified by idleness. The person is able to watch work but not get involved. They enjoy work as long as others do it. God says an idle soul is going to suffer hunger. That sounds like a degree of poverty. They are the kind of person that thinks the weather is never right for doing anything.

The starving of the world need to realize the necessity to work long and hard. That would solve much of their poverty. Do you realize that the Indians of the Great Plains (the bread basket of America – Iowa, Nebraska, Kansas, and South Dakota) spent most of their time being hungry because they didn't think it was a fit thing for a human to grow a garden? They thought that anyone could grow a garden because it was easy. Instead, they preferred to sit and wait for the buffalo to come by and decide to hunt it. When they got one, they let a lot of it rot, stuffing their bellies but not saving any of it. The ground that it took to support one Indian can support a thousand people today by being farmed. The problem was idleness and that leads to hunger.

Proverbs 12:27 says,

> *"The slothful man roasteth not that which he took in hunting: but the substance of a diligent man is precious."*

Notice that the slothful doesn't appreciate or value what he does have. He may say, "All I got was a rabbit, and I was looking for a deer." Make some rabbit stew, but don't throw the rabbit out. Then when you get the deer you will know how to appreciate it. The diligent looks at what he has and realizes it is precious because he does have something.

Proverbs 13:4 says,

> *"The soul of the sluggard desireth, and hath nothing: but the soul of the diligent shall be made fat."*

They are in similar circumstances, but the one prospers while the other suffers. The slothful is always wanting while the diligent learn to make do with what they have and perhaps produce something more.

Most of the advertising in America is to make people slothful and dissatisfied. They say, "You have labored hard 40 hours this week, you deserve a break." Where in the world did we get the idea that 40 hours was all that we are supposed to put in? The Bible says, "Six days shalt thou labor..." (Exodus 20:9). Then we

CHAPTER 14: SLOTHFULNESS

have some people from outside our country who will work for fewer wages on jobs that we are not even interested in. They get along living in parts of town that we wouldn't count worth living in. Then their grandchildren end up owning our homes, buying our farms, and owning our businesses. Some are diligent and the others are slothful. We have been living on desires and they have been living on work, learning to value whatever they have. They end up being made fat, and we go hungry. We can't figure it out. We think that the answer is to keep immigrants out of our country. It is a matter of what a person makes of what they have, rather than what they grumble about and desire to have. Sometimes it is those desires and wishes that will destroy us.

Proverbs 20:4 says,

> *"The sluggard will not plow by reason of the cold; therefore shall he beg in the harvest, and have nothing."*

The slothful man says, "I know it is the time of year to put out a field, but it is still too cold to do anything." The next morning he thinks it is too chilly to start, and the following day he says it looks like rain. On and on it goes. By the time they get to it, if they ever do, there is not enough growing season left for them to have any harvest. Consequently, they are the ones begging and trying to get others to feel sorry for them.

They are waiting for that easy job that pays well. Most people that I meet are looking for big money for easy work. Let me tell you a little secret – if there were big money for easy work, somebody else would already have the job. The big money is always for hardwork and the easy work is the kind that pays so little nobody else wanted it. Somehow, the slothful person cannot grasp that and is waiting for the big bucks to land in his lap for a little effort.

Proverbs 21:25 says,

> "The desire of the slothful killeth him: for his hands refuse to labour."

He has all these great desires and plans, all these things that he wants to accomplish, but he is hoping somehow that "his ship is going to come in." He just can't get himself to do the work that it takes to produce it. That is the mark of the slothful – always wanting, but not doing.

Proverbs 24:30-32 says,

> "I went by the field of the slothful, and by the vineyard of the man void of understanding; And, lo, it was all grown over with thorns, and nettles had covered the face thereof, and the stone wall thereof was broken down. Then I saw, and considered it well: I looked upon it, and received instruction."

I remember working for an old German man named Mr. Bull. I only worked one day for him, and after that day, I understood why he was so rich. He expected much and gave little. His wife paid better wages so I went to work for her and kept her garden. He asked me to pick some cherries on a farm he had out in the country. We headed out to the farm at about 20 miles an hour. That was at the time when the speed limit was 60 mph. When he got out to some cornfields, he slowed down even more and I wondered if I just got out and walked if I couldn't get there faster. He was looking as he drove and drew my attention to a field, commenting that if the owner would put tile in his field he would be able to increase his harvest. There had been water that had laid in that area in the spring which was why the corn wasn't doing well. He concluded by saying that the man was not going to invest anything in his fields. We went a little further and he

CHAPTER 14: SLOTHFULNESS

pointed to some cows. They belonged to the same farmer and he wasn't about to fix his fence even though he might lose his cows or corn or both. We were observing a farmer that was slothful. I think in the back of his mind, Mr. Bull thought that if he waited a few more years the farmer would be so broke that he would be able to buy his farm. I am not sure that he even knew the Biblical principles, but he understood it in practice. If you don't take care of your land, your land won't take care of you.

Further, if you don't take care of your job, your job won't be there to take care of you. That is why many companies go under. Their employees are like the city man who owned a horse and complained to a farmer that it was too expensive to feed him. He told the farmer that he had about solved the problem so that he could feed his horse cheaply. He said he had started mixing a little sawdust with the oats – just a little bit – and the horse didn't notice it at first. Then each day he put a little more sawdust in and a little less oats. He complained, "Do you know that I about had that horse weaned from oats to sawdust, when he up and died on me?" Do you know that there are numerous employees that have just about figured out how not to work, when all of a sudden the job shuts down, and they can't figure out what went wrong.

Take a look at slothfulness all around you and learn a lesson from it. If you won't receive instruction from looking at the slothful, you will become such yourself, and you will suffer the same consequences. I am not suggesting being critical of them, just learn from them so that you don't make the same mistakes and pay the same price.

Look at **Proverbs 26:13**,

> *"The slothful man saith, There is a lion in the way; a lion is in the streets."*

No doubt that is reason enough to stay home from work for the day.

Old King Saul had a problem with a giant named Goliath one day. His servants came bringing a little shepherd boy into his court. The shepherd boy offered to take care of the giant. Saul wanted to know how he intended to do that. David recounted that one day while he was watching the sheep, along came a bear, and he killed it. There was another day that there was a lion. Now the slothful says that there is a lion in the streets – but David saw the lion in his field. That is even closer, isn't it? Did he go home for the day and knock off work? Did he tell the sheep to watch out for themselves because he was taking care of #1? Isn't that what many people think? David took care of a lion so that he could take care of a giant. Eventually he cared for a country.

Proverbs 26:14 says,

> "As the door turneth upon his hinges, so doth the slothful upon his bed."

Back and forth.

Proverbs 26:15 says,

> "The slothful hideth his hand in his bosom; it grieveth him to bring it again to his mouth."

It is all he can do just to feed himself, much less produce the food. He thinks it is a great thing that he fed himself. Can you picture this? These are the ones that think they have done something great when they have just provided for their needs by the sweat of the brow of others.

The next verse, **16** says,

> "The sluggard is wiser in his own conceit than

CHAPTER 14: SLOTHFULNESS

seven men that can render a reason."

In other words, you are not going to be able to out-argue the sluggard. You can take seven men who have a good reason to talk to the slothful man and straighten him out, but in his own conceit, he is smarter than all seven of them. There is not much hope for the sluggard because you can't talk or explain to him. He thinks he knows more than all of the rest put together.

The sluggard looks at the difficulties instead of the opportunities. Do you remember when God opened up the Red Sea for the Israelites? They went through and a little bit later went up to Kadesh Barnea and God said, "There's the land, go get it." They wanted to see what it was like so that they knew what they were getting. Ten of the twelve spies did not see what they were really getting; they just saw what was in the way. When they came back, they said that there were giants. But really, what they were saying was that there were *"lion(s) in the streets."* They looked at the difficulties, but Joshua and Caleb tried to get them to see the opportunities and look at God. The people focused on the difficulty, and they were only permitted to partake of the grapes of Eschol that got carried back. They were stuck with manna for forty more years. They looked at the difficulties and wouldn't buy up the opportunity. It is so easy to do that.

WHAT IS THE CURE?

Be active at work despite the problems. Do the best and the most that you can. I know that will get some of you in trouble with the union stewards. Learn to value your work however big or little it might be. It might be an opossum that you get while you are hunting, but roast opossum is better than an empty stomach. Learn to be diligent and accomplish what you can. Don't be slothful. Accomplish what is possible and see what God does with that.

CHAPTER 15

IGNORING THE NEEDS OF THE POOR

Proverbs 21:13 says,

> "Whoso stoppeth his ears at the cry of the poor, he also shall cry himself, but shall not be heard."

Ignoring the needs of the poor brings poverty. I emphasize the word "needs." Ignoring their needs is a very self-centered and coldhearted way to live. We are forgetting that "others" might be "us" one day. If we ignore their cry, our cry shall not be heard. God says that you reap what you sow.

WHAT IS THE CURE?

The obvious cure is to help the poor.

Look at **Proverbs 28:27**,

> "He that giveth unto the poor shall not lack: but he that hideth his eyes shall have many a curse."

This is a promise. Those that always want to receive but never give are going to lack, but those that give will not lack. A word of caution on learning how to help the poor: make sure you help them, and don't just appease or satisfy them in the immediate, temporary situation.

Let me give you a classic example in the Bible of those that would not help the poor and literally were destroyed because of it. In **Ezekiel 16:48, 49** we see an explanation of something from the book of Genesis about Sodom and Gomorrah. It says,

> "As I live, saith the Lord God, Sodom thy sister

> *hath not done, she nor her daughters, as thou hast done, thou and thy daughters. Behold, this was the iniquity of thy sister Sodom, pride, fulness of bread, and abundance of idleness was in her and in her daughters, neither did she strengthen the hand of the poor and needy."*

Now everybody knows what Sodom is known for, and we are all sure we know why God was going to destroy it. But I want you to look at what God says was the iniquity of Sodom and why He had to destroy it:

1. "Pride"
2. "Fullness of bread"
3. "Abundance of idleness was in her and in her daughters."

You thought it was homosexuality, didn't you? How many homosexuals are busy working all the time? Idleness is the Devil's playground. Think about it. These root causes permitted that promiscuous sexual conduct in that city. We look at the symptoms, and God looks at the causes. As America has built herself up full of pride, fullness of bread, and abundance of idleness, it is no wonder that we have the result of Sodom. If you look at the last part of verse 49 it says,

> *"Neither did she strengthen the hand of the poor and needy."*

She had the poor and needy but never did anything to get them back on their feet. She didn't do anything to meet their need or really help them. America is in the same place.

If you ignore the need of the poor, one day you will become poor yourself. What are the needs of the poor? They need to have their hands strengthened. The old proverb:

CHAPTER 15: IGNORING THE NEEDS OF THE POOR

> "It is better to teach a man how to fish than to give him some to eat"

is not a Bible verse, but there is Bible teaching behind it. Help them to provide. Meet their needs. Help them, don't just carry them. The result will be that we all are better off.

CHAPTER 16

LOVE OF PLEASURE

Proverbs 21:17a says,

"He that loveth pleasure shall be a poor man:"

One of the causes of poverty is a love of pleasure. That is, constantly seeking pleasure, desiring to be pleased, and having all kinds of exterior excitements fed into your life makes for poverty. It has become so bad that when some churches advertise services, you would think that they were copying Barnum and Bailey Circus. They have the smallest dwarf preaching the Gospel. What that has to do with the message I haven't figured out yet. The preacher is going to swallow a goldfish – but the circus will have them swallow a sword! I am surprised they haven't brought in some Siamese twins to sing a duet. I knew of one place where they even brought an elephant on the platform. One place was going to have the world's biggest milkshake stirred with an outboard motor. People go running for it because they love pleasure. Do you know what will happen? They will all end up poor and not just spiritually poor either.

Somehow or another we have gotten the idea that pleasures and the love of pleasures are to be pampered, encouraged, and built up. I believe that we ought to make a joyful noise unto the Lord, but the world has enough amusement parks and pleasure rides. This will make some poor while others become rich from people seeking pleasure. You don't have to look far in any newspaper to find someone advertising some sort of pleasure in order to get your money.

Christians are getting caught up in this type of thing. It is amazing the time given to pleasure, the amount of energy and money poured out for pleasures, and the place that it occupies in their thoughts. Often they measure that which they count worthwhile in their lives by whether it pleases them, rather than whether it pleases God.

WHAT IS THE CURE?

Get serious about life. Shakespeare said,

> "All the world is a stage and men and women are merely players." (Shakespeare's *As You Like It*, Act II, Scene vii)

America says that all of life is a game and we are to have much fun and pleasure before we die. The Bible states that there are some who would say, *"...eat, drink, and be merry"* (Luke 12:19b). I have never recommended that kind of philosophy.

Some people love pleasures in the cheap way and others in the expensive way, according to what they have available to them. Still, it is a way to poverty just as much as being slothful and never earning any money. Some people can earn big money and spend it just as quickly on pleasure. All they have are empty memories and an appetite that was not satisfied but desires even more and more pleasures. They are just as broke as before they earned that money. Some of you have been delivered from this, but let me sound a word of warning – past deliverance does not guarantee future safety.

CHAPTER 17

SPENDING IT UP

Proverbs 21:20 says,

> *"There is treasure to be desired and oil in the dwelling of the wise; but a foolish man spendeth it up."*

"Spendeth it up" is talking about spending everything you have. You may have a certain amount, and you spend it all. As soon as many people realize they are going to get a little more, they have already figured out how to spend it. In fact, they have figured how they are going to spend more than they are going to get, and then have to make choices. You have seen a little child who has a quarter "burning a hole in his pocket", just itching to spend it. Well, most people think that money is only to be spent, and they don't realize there may be other Biblical uses for it. The foolish man spends everything he gets – never saving just spending and spending.

In fact, some even go a little further and try to spend more than they have. If a foolish man spends it all, what in the world does it mean for those that spend more? Somehow, they believe that things will always get better and because they are going to get better, they can care for these other things in the future. They ignore the Scriptural teaching that things are going to "wax worse and worse" (**II Timothy 3:13**: *But evil men and seducers shall wax worse and worse, deceiving, and being deceived*.). They believe their "ship is going to come in" or they are going to find the end of their rainbow. Everything will get solved all at once. If God solved some people's problems all at once, they would just go out and do the same thing again. God lets us get out slowly. Why?

Because that is how you got in, and He doesn't want you going back to the same thing again.

The concept behind spending it all up is – "I'm going to live as high as I possibly can financially. I want to live at the highest level of society that I can stretch my money to. I am going to look as good and live as comfortably and leisurely as possible." This is absolutely out of step with the living of the Lord Jesus Christ Who left everything in heaven and became poor for our sakes that we might be able to have the spiritual wealth that He gave.

> *"The foxes have holes, and the birds of the air have nests; but the Son of man hath not where to lay His head"* **(Matthew 8:20).**

When it came time to pay taxes, He sent Peter to catch a fish that had enough money in his mouth to pay taxes for the two of them.

Proverbs 6:6 says,

> *"Go to the ant, thou sluggard; consider her ways, and be wise:"*

Learn how the ant labors in the summer so that it has provisions in the winter. We live as high as we can possibly get away with, yet we expect missionaries to do without due to our wasteful living. We feel it is spiritual to be poor. To demand that the ambassador be poor so that the supporter can be rich and the ambassador can be spiritual, means that you want to be unspiritual. That tells you something about your heart.

> *"Pride goeth before destruction…"* **(Proverbs 16:18).**

> *"God resisteth the proud"* **(James 4:6).**

CHAPTER 17: SPENDING IT UP

WHAT IS THE CURE?

Somehow, learn to spend less than you make. I know that sounds un-American, but it is Biblical. Learn how to live below your means. You will have to be alert to advertisements because they have sold you on living above your means. Learn how to save some, if it is no more than a dollar here and there. Maybe some weeks you'll be able to do more.

God took this verse and began to plow in my heart. My wife was wise in this area, and I was the foolish one. I found out that when things were tight I wondered how we were going to make it; I was still able to save a dollar that week. Then I had it for when I needed it later.

Brother Steven Worth helped me a lot with this. His father ran a truck farm, and they grew vegetables for Philadelphia. His daddy gave him a five dollar bill and then told him to keep it in his wallet. It was his, but he wasn't to spend it, unless it was an absolute emergency that his father would understand. If I remember the story right, he did that for each of his boys. He carried that bill until it got moldy. He would add a little of his own money here and there, but he learned that somehow you can carry money without having to spend it. A strange idea, but it is Biblical. He said that learning how to carry money without spending it was an excellent financial lesson to him.

Spending it up is part of our very nature as Americans. That is how we think. "If I have it, I will spend it. If I don't then I will have to wait till I get it, and then I'll spend it." The idea of spending less than we have seems strange to us – sort of like punishment. Let me say that there is a freedom when you learn to live below your means that those who live above their means will never know. How can I say that? I have been both places. Hold some back for those needs and emergencies that come.

CHAPTER 18

BORROWING MONEY

Proverbs 22:7 says,

> *"The rich ruleth over the poor, and the borrower is servant to the lender."*

The next cause logically follows. Borrowing money is another cause of poverty. Have you ever noticed that when you walk into a bank to open a savings account or to get a certificate of deposit that they act differently than when you ask to take out a loan? In fact, you would think that you were in two different banks.

Borrowing money is a form of slavery. You have obligated so many hours, days, weeks, months, or years of your life to someone else. This is measured by how long it will take you to get it paid back. If a person ever has to borrow money, he ought to make a careful choice on who his slave master will be. He should also consider whether he needs the money enough to go into that kind of bondage for it.

Do you realize that a part of slavery in America was by choice and never forced? There were poor people in the Old Country who would sell themselves as slaves to a plantation owner, businessman, or tradesman for a certain number of years and the master would pay off all their debts. The master would bring them over to the colonies, house, feed, and care for them and at the end of that time, was obligated to give them at least a mule or plow, a shovel or hoe, and a certain amount of food and seed. Then they would move up into the mountain areas where they were able to do some homesteading and get started on their own. It was the only way out of a financial bondage that some of them had, so they chose to become "indentured servants."

CAUSES AND CURES OF POVERTY

People ask me whether I own my house and I tell them that the bank and I do. As far as I am concerned, we are working in a partnership and I am buying them out. I can always sell out, pay them off, and still have something left. Some people have literally "sold their soul to the company store." Only it is the bank or some other individual. This form of slavery is hard to get free of. If you are not careful, you are going to borrow to make payments on what you borrowed. Uncle Sam has been trying that trick for a while.

A person ought to solemnly consider that when they borrow, what they are actually doing is not only spending it all up, but choosing to live above their means for a little while. Then they will have to live below their means for a long time. A person that borrows $1,000 so they can live that much higher is going to have to live $1,000 below their income later to pay it back, plus who knows how much interest. They might end up living below their income $2,000 so that they could live $1,000 above it for a little while.

Here is a question about borrowing I ask myself from time to time. I don't like to answer it, but it has saved me from some financial insanity on occasions. If you can't afford to pay for it now, how are you going to pay for it later and the interest besides? Think about it. You may pay for it twice with the interest involved. We are in such a "hurry up" to get, that we never think about the "slow down" to pay. If you can afford to pay for it now, why don't you just pay for it now instead of borrowing? If you have good answers to those questions – okay, but if you don't, they may slow you down a little.

Years ago, I stayed in the home of a friend who was a public accountant. He brought his computer home and was showing me a little about it. He figured what it would cost to borrow $50,000 for a 30 year mortgage given the interest rates at the time. Then

CHAPTER 18: BORROWING MONEY

we took that payment and programmed it back in to figure out that if a person puts that same amount of money in the bank every month, and was able to get a good interest rate on it, how long it would take until he would have $50,000. To pay the bank back it would take 30 years, but to invest that same payment you would have $50,000 in between five and six years. That is where the rich get richer and the poor get poorer. I had thought it would take about 10 years, but when I found out it would only take five or six years, I became angry. If you could learn to live below your means a whole lot now, then you could live above your means a whole lot later.

WHAT IS THE CURE?

Learn to save ahead for your needs. Imagine if someone could start saving a monthly payment on a house for five or six years. They would be ready to cash buy instead of having to borrow for 30 years to pay for it. Then if they wanted, they could start payments again, putting it back into the bank and saving it up. Five or six years later, they could buy a second house and rent that one out, adding the rent to the payments they had been making. Then by the end of the 30 years, they could own something like eight or ten houses. Or if they just wanted to start out buying to begin with they would own one at the end of the 30 years.

You wonder how the banks can afford to cash build all these branches. It is no problem – you are paying for them. Learn to pay for your needs. Learn that a little done without now has great benefits later. Learn to count the cost. And if you are in this bondage, as most everybody finds themselves, learn to somehow live below what means you have so you can buy yourself out of slavery.

Do you realize that there were instances in the North and

South during the times of slavery that a slave would come to the auction block and when the bidding was done the slave had saved enough with little bits of work here and there, that he was able to buy his own freedom? They bid for themselves, and bought their own freedom.

Wouldn't you like to buy out from under slavery? If the borrower is servant to the lender, you can buy your financial freedom. The secret of it is, that the sooner you get started the easier it is going to get. But the longer you wait the deeper you will be and the higher the price will be. The Bible says that the *"righteous considereth the cause of the poor,"* but the world is just going to stay poor and blame someone else for it. Imagine somebody handling a million dollars in a lifetime and never being able to get out of debt. You see, the world has lived a little below their means so they could lend money to the Lord's church and His people – and now they own us.

You ought to see the amusement on people's faces when I tell them we have built a church building without borrowing a nickel. They wonder how a church can do that. They thought we were all so poor that we ought to belong to the bank. Then the bank would decide when we would get the money to build. Some of these national religious figures, the best known of your T.V. personalities, have had all of the financial decisions of their church and television ministries put into a receivership. This means that the judge said he wanted some of the business men of their community that were not connected with their church in any way to decide how the offerings of that church would be spent until they could get straightened up financially. The world owned them.

Some churches have borrowed from different organizations that they didn't agree with at all. They then found out they couldn't speak about what they believed in on certain subjects

CHAPTER 18: BORROWING MONEY

because they would have been forced into immediate bankruptcy. Because of debt, the church is losing control of where it is and what it can do. The same thing can happen in an individual's life. They can attach your wages before you get to take any money out to give, if you get a little behind or violate one of those minor sentences in that long document that you signed to be able to get the money to live higher than you could afford.

It is amazing how spiritual we are until it comes to our money. Christians that would like to give far more are paying out hundreds and thousands of dollars a year in interest that could have been given to God's work. Just take a look at your income tax report and see what you had at the end of the year. See whether you were satisfied to finance the bank rather than the work of Jesus Christ with that amount of interest. I have to look at it every year and consider it and it is sobering.

The U.S. laws allow for bankruptcy or rule to escape the payment of just debts or the payment of debts on time. But God's Word knows no such laws. Those laws were put into effect and practiced originally by those who rejected the Word of God. Many Christians are running to them as a cure for their disobedience rather than repentance and making of restitution. I read of a case where a man was forced into bankruptcy. He didn't choose it and fought against it. But his creditors sued and forced him into bankruptcy and then took everything that he had. He had spent the last 10 or 12 years paying back what the government said he didn't owe anymore. He said that he was Christian and believed he owed it anyway. He has been working to pay it back, and he will continue to work to pay back all that the government let him off with in court.

Many people will use legal means to escape Biblical responsibility. But I want you to know that just because our

Congress passed a law doesn't mean that God agreed with it. There is a heavenly court that has to be faced. This court ranks far above that of the Supreme Court and we must live by that decision. The matter of borrowing money is a dangerous thing. We need to learn to save for our needs, do without, count the cost, and get our freedom back instead of selling ourselves out to the world and letting them run our lives.

CHAPTER 19

OPPRESSION OF THE POOR

Proverbs 22:16 says,

> *"He that oppresseth the poor to increase his riches, and he that giveth to the rich, shall surely come to want."*

(There are two here – we will deal with the first one and then move on to the second.)

First, the oppression of the poor to become wealthy is a cause of poverty. Those that are poor will be quick to tell you who takes advantage of them and helps keep them poor. They use them somehow to be able to make more money than is necessary. They view the poor as foolish and in a bind, so they can take advantage of their poverty and are able to line their own pockets and increase their riches. God says that there will come a time when they will come to want.

How do they do this? Sometimes they take advantage of the ignorance of the poor or their lack of proper understanding. I have worked with poor people who have been manipulated legally because they didn't have enough education to understand documents they signed or know whether legal matters were properly carried out. They have had me look at things such as contracts. Then when I explained what the contract said they remarked that was not what they were told. Then they realized that someone was trying to take advantage of them. It happens all the time.

For a few beads and bangles, we bought Manhattan Island. That was taking advantage of those poor Indians, wasn't it? We swapped great farmland for the desert land with those Indians. Then we got upset when we found out that that they had oil under those deserts. We tried to figure some way to get the oil from them too. That is oppressing the poor.

People may be in a financial bind, and that is a great chance for a loan shark to jump in and hit them with high interest, just until they get their next check. Making them work for less than what they are worth is another example of oppressing the poor. God says that the wages that are kept back, cry out to God before Him, and they become a canker to the rich (James 5:1-6).

The rent that is charged is another way of oppressing the poor. I am amazed at the rent poor people pay that those who are better off would never pay for even a nicer place. Somehow, they are bound into the poverty trap. Slumlords take advantage of them for everything they can. Transportation can be taken advantage of too.

I am not saying that a poor person should not have to carry his load, but we are not to take advantage of him in order to line our pockets. Some people sell particularly to the poor knowing that they can make a quick sale. God flatly condemns the oppression of the poor constantly throughout the Scriptures. He says there is a curse on those that make their money from the poor. There will come a time when those who do this will be in want somehow.

If you study the history of the making of millions of some families in America, you will understand why they lost it all somewhere along the line. Somewhere they made it the wrong way. When you make it wrong, God says that you are going to lose it, even if it is a generation or two down the road.

CHAPTER 19: OPPRESSION OF THE POOR

WHAT IS THE CURE?

Learn to be merciful to the poor. Learn to help them. Don't try to make that little extra from them. Don't see them as an easy target for the lining of your pockets. It doesn't mean that you can't make a right profit from them, and it doesn't mean that you deal with a slack hand towards them. That will never help them. There is a difference between helping the poor and just giving to them. They need help more than they need gifts. They will never get on their feet if they don't get the help.

CHAPTER 20

GIVING GIFTS TO THE RICH

There is a second cause found in **Proverbs 22:16**,

> *"He that giveth to the rich, shall surely come to want."*

The giving of gifts to the rich is an easy way to go broke. After all, you are not going to be able to give cheap gifts to rich people and get very far. If you are giving it to the rich people to try to impress them, it probably won't because they are already rich. What you have to offer them is not going to excite them, add to their pride, or enrich them a whole lot. But it is going to cost you a great deal in the process.

If you want to make this a "double whammy" – borrow money to try to buy a gift to give the rich. That will really catch you coming and going. Try to buy the friendship of the rich and you may find that it is not for sale. They have a lot of other people trying the same stunt. If you are trying to get an inside track with them, or to obligate them to you, you may want to consider why they are rich. Among other things, they learned not to give gifts to the rich. They kept it for themselves. Have you ever noticed that some rich people don't just "give out" so loosely? Some people get so involved in giving gifts to those that don't need them that they work hard all year to pay for the gifts they give.

WHAT IS THE CURE?

Instead of giving gifts to the rich, learn to hang onto it for your own needs or perhaps give it to a poor person. It is amazing the two things that are tied together in this verse - oppressing the poor and giving gifts to the rich. If anything, you ought to make your money from the rich and give something to help the poor. That would be Biblical. Make it from those that have, so you can give it to those that do not.

I saw a man who makes his money in this way, giving a water heater to someone who needed it instead of selling it. He said he wanted to give it to them and wouldn't let them pay for it. He knew that it wouldn't help him get to heaven and that he needed to repent of his sins, but it still make him feel good by giving to the poor. He said he would rather give to a poor person than to give something to a rich man. That man understood more Bible than many church people. He didn't know that principle was in the Bible, but God had revealed something to the man's heart.

He that gives to the poor having made it from the rich is the one that won't have any want. Think about the absolute foolishness of some people's thinking. They want to make a whole lot from where there is not much – the poor. Then they want to dump it off where there is a whole lot. Any farmer that thought like that would go broke. If he had a good field and a bad field, then spent all of his time in the bad field taking whatever he could get out of that and investing it back into the good field, but never doing anything with the good field, he would never make it.

CHAPTER 21

DRUNKENNESS

Proverbs 23:21 says,

"For the drunkard and the glutton shall come to poverty: and drowsiness shall clothe a man with rags."

What ways are there to get drunk? Proverbs 21:17 talks about those that "love wine" and what happens to them. There are some people that develop a love for liquor and wine in particular. I have not had the unfortunate situation of being a connoisseur in this area. But I know that the odor of most whiskey and beer doesn't really make me thirsty for it. If odor has anything to do with the taste, I think a taste would have to be developed.

Liquor of one form or another can cause drunkenness, but a person can get drunk without liquor. The verse doesn't say that they were drunk on wine and strong drink. Let me suggest that a person can get drunk from drugs, with no alcohol involved. Drunkenness is a state where a person is not in control of his mind. Senses are dulled and reality is no longer real. Most people that I have met that get drunk on drugs, liquor, or anything else don't get drunk just to get drunk. Some do, but some get drunk to get mean. A few get drunk so they can get into a fight or get their courage up. But most get drunk to escape reality. They don't want to face what really is.

Gambling is another thing that will cause drunkenness. I remember going to visit Mr. Riley one wet, rainy night. I drove my car as far up in the driveway as was safe and then trudged through the mud the rest of the way to a trailer home in Pinhook

Hollow just down the road from where I lived in Sinking Springs, Ohio. I was going to see Tom Riley about his soul. I knocked on the door. When they saw who I was, I guess they felt sorry for the wet duck and let me in. I stood there dripping wet and cold and they went ahead and finished out the hand of poker they were playing. They started another one while I just stood there and prayed. They began to get upset, and nobody was happy about how that hand was going. I think they hoped I would leave and I hoped they would quit. As I stood around that table watching them play, they weren't drunk on liquor or drugs, but they were drunk on gambling. They weren't in the real world. They weren't concerned about their soul. They weren't concerned about their bills, sickness, or anything except which card they were going to get next and which card was going down on the table. I waited longer than they could wait and I finally got to talk to him about his soul. Several years later, he came to me and said that God had dealt with him and he wanted to be saved, although I fear that he never was.

Those of you who have gambled know what I am talking about. If you have shot crap, you know that those little black spots that were coming up on top of a little white cube were more important to you than what Russia, Washington, and Britain did combined. You were living in an unreal world. If it was betting on ball games you didn't care whether income taxes went up or down, but rather who got the most points in that game. A game was no longer a game. It became an all-consuming passion. You became as drunk as a drunk got on liquor. The world calls them gambleholics now.

There are those that become drunk on pleasures. One of the most futile things that I know of is to try to talk soberly to people about their soul in the middle of an amusement park. Those people are as drunk as if you were trying to talk to them at a bar. You must get them away to talk much sense to them.

CHAPTER 21: DRUNKENNESS

I used to think that the place that I would want the Lord to send me least (and He knows I am willing) was New York City. But I think that I have found another place instead. That is Florida. I know every preacher wants to go to Florida, at least in the winter. But I pity the poor preachers down there. One preacher that I had heard of was trying to hold the line and preach something straight just a few miles from Disney World, Circus World, Sea World, and a whole lot of other worldly-like things. I am not saying that a person should never go to such places, but he had to live there and minister to the people that lived in that atmosphere. He is gone from that church now partly because he was preaching too strong. Those people were pleasure minded down there. I am talking about people that have retired from their jobs in the North and retired from God and church. Many have gone down there just to have a good time for the rest of their lives. I know that there are some saved people there, but I am talking about the general atmosphere throughout the cities and towns. They are as drunk as anybody that had to be helped staggering from a bar. They will come to poverty because they are eating up what they earned all those years.

There is another kind of drunkenness that I'm concerned about, and that is drunkenness on power. Some people get power and it goes to their head so they can't think straight. Some people get promoted above their abilities. The best thing that can happen to them is to get demoted, because they have more power and prestige than they can handle. They think they have become an authority on everything, and that they don't have to listen to anybody.

Some folks can handle a promotion, and some can handle many promotions, but others do best never to take one. That is all it takes to ruin them. Some of you have had friends that ceased to be friends when they got one step too high. They didn't know you anymore. They couldn't talk or think the same, or even look at things the same. They were drunk on power.

Now the verse speaks of the drunkard. That person that not only gets drunk once, but keeps getting drunk again and again. The drunkard – whether it is the one that keeps getting drunk on liquor, or high on drugs, or becomes wrapped up in his gambling pleasures, or power again and again – if he continues on that road he will go broke. He will be poor. This is not talking about the person that was drunk once, but rather the person that allowed this to become a way of life for him. It dulls the senses, wastes the money, and makes for an unreal thought life. That will bring him to poverty sooner or later.

I don't know whether you have ever been around men in rescue missions and talked to them much. I realize that some of them are excellent con artists and liars, but have you ever noticed that they are not usually people that have been poor all their lives? One may have owned a dry cleaning business or some restaurants, and another may have been a professor at a university. It wasn't the education that got them in a rescue mission. It wasn't that they had never made money. Why are they so poor? Drunkenness is one of the answers. Drunkenness literally brought them to the bottom of things. We get to thinking that drunkards are that way just because they have never had anything, but that is not so. If I could somehow take you, with the eye of an angel, down to the rich parts of town, and have you look into the hearts and lives of the people there, you would find some drunks. They are not all in the poor sections yet. Drunkenness is not a respecter of your bank account, your education, or you position in society – it will bring you to poverty.

WHAT IS THE CURE?

Stay sober. Do you know how not to get drunk on liquor? Don't drink it. I have never heard of anyone who got drunk on

CHAPTER 21: DRUNKENNESS

liquor that never had a drink. That is the easiest way to stay sober. You may think you can drink a certain amount but when you get about half of that in you, you think that you can drink more than you did when you were sober. It is amazing that with most people, the more they drink, the more they think they can drink.

The person on drugs may think that just one reef with a little bit of pot in it is not going to hurt him. Then he gets that one and wants two more. Then he wants something stronger, etc.

Some may say that they can bet a quarter on a game. You better hope you lose it, because if you win on a quarter bet, you will risk a dollar. If you win on a dollar, a ten-spot is next. The high-rollers were not always the losers. The reason that they are rolling high on the big bets is because they won on the little bets. They keep thinking they are always going to win. Those casinos spot such when they walk in, and they let them win a little here and there so they can get all the rest of what they have.

Be careful in these areas, and don't even dabble in these things.

CHAPTER 22

GLUTTONY

There is a second cause in the same verse, **Proverbs 23:21**,

"...The glutton shall come to poverty:"

I am amazed at the pride in gluttony that is openly boasted about in Christian circles today. People brag about how much food they can consume, as if that is a spiritual statement. I believe in feasting as well as fasting, but some people think it is always feasting, and that can lead to gluttony. Let me say quickly that gluttony has to do with overeating and not necessarily being overweight. Some of the greatest gluttons that I have known were underweight. I don't know why, but the only thing I can figure is that they used all their energy just digesting what they ate. Maybe they had so punished their system that it just didn't digest and only passed through. But I will be honest, I ate far more when I was underweight than I do now when I am overweight.

Gluttony is the punishing of yourself by pouring food in, continually stashing, stowing, and forcing it down. God says the glutton is going to come to poverty. How will it cause him to come to poverty?

The cost of the food will affect him. Look at how much money he is eating up in food. On the authority of the Word of God, Jesus expects the saved to fast from time to time. The money saved from the expense of the food can be used more wisely somewhere else.

The time spent eating could have been used better. When you could have eaten a normal amount in 30 minutes, and you took an hour to eat twice as much, you just lost thirty minutes. If you did that twice a day, that is 365 hours in a year. That is an equivalent of a little over nine weeks of work spent at the table unnecessarily. What would you have done with an extra nine weeks of pay? That could help you get out of poverty.

Then there is the matter that overeating slows the body processes down. If you will look at the verse – "For the drunkard and the glutton shall come to poverty: and drowsiness shall clothe a man with rags." There is a relationship here. The body processes of those who get high on drugs, get drunk all the time, live for pleasures, gamble all the time or are gluttons are affected, and they can't work like they normally could have. Their body is slowed down by the damage that is done by these things. They are not able to produce as much, and it has a drowsy effect on their life. If you have ever fasted at any length, you will find that sometimes you can get by on a half hour's less sleep a day when you're fasting, but when you are feasting you need an hour's extra sleep a day to make it. That drowsy effect factors in.

Another way gluttony causes poverty is the issue of sickness as the body is punished by having more than is necessary poured into it. Sickness can get expensive particularly in the latter days of a person's life when things go wrong from this abuse.

WHAT IS THE CURE?

Learn to eat sensibly. Feast on occasion, and fast on occasion. Be sensible the rest of the time. Learn that you are to eat to live and not live to eat. Some people literally live from one meal time to the next. I'm not talking about starving people, but rather some people whose whole life is so wrapped up in food that mealtimes are the high points of their lives. Recognize that food is a necessity of life, but it is only to help us live and should not be the goal of our lives.

CHAPTER 23

VAIN FRIENDS

Proverbs 28:19 says,

> "He that tilleth his land shall have plenty of bread: but he that followeth after vain persons shall have poverty enough."

The picture here is of a farmer – maybe a young farm boy that has inherited the farm and now has to decide whether to spend his time working the fields or running around with his friends in town. Sometimes the reason a farmer loses his farm is that he didn't take time enough to farm it. A man doesn't work a farm in 40 hours a week. He is glad during the slow times in the winter to only have to work 70 and 80 hours a week, so he can rest up for the busy times. He learns to till and work those fields to the fullest.

The principle is this: If you follow vain people, you will go broke. Wrong friends can lead you to poverty. There is a parallel verse in **Proverbs 12:11**,

> "He that tilleth his land shall be satisfied with bread: but he that followeth vain persons is void of understanding."

Not only is he going to have poverty, but he lacks understanding. If you run with the wrong kind of friends, you will end up thinking wrong because you will learn to think like they do. Not only do "birds of a feather flock together," but you will become one of those birds if you are around them long enough. You need to be selective in choosing friends in terms of what you want.

You will pick up not only the thought patterns but also the attitudes of those that you are around. I can talk to a person and get a good idea of what their friends are like just by listening to them a while. We echo our friends more than we realize.

Wrong friends also make for wasted time, as they will absorb great amounts of time. That will lead you to poverty too. Some so-called friends are like leeches. They soak up the energy and time that should have been spent doing something else. Friends that care about you will care about your time. People that don't care about your time aren't really your friends. They will not only take away your time, but will waste your opportunities. You won't see those opportunities again, you will become negative in your thinking, and everything will become a problem. You will forget that every problem is a potential opportunity in disguise. All you will see are the problems. You will become a complainer like they are.

Not only that, they will help you spend what you do have of money. Look at the prodigal son – he had friends only while he had money. They took up his time, and they affected his thinking and attitudes. They wasted his opportunities and spent his money. Then when he had nothing, they left him to go watch the hogs. The Jewish people weren't to have anything to do with those unclean animals and there he was, out there wishing he could just slop at the trough with the hogs. If you have ever seen hogs eat, or fed them, you know that prodigal son was in bad shape. I have never seen anything in a hog trough that made me hungry!

WHAT IS THE CURE?

Select your friends very carefully. Keep a watch, or they will drain you until you are just skin and bones, and then dump you. That will cause poverty.

CHAPTER 24

GET RICH QUICK SCHEMES

Proverbs 28:22 says,

> *"He that hasteth to be rich hath an evil eye, and considereth not that poverty shall come upon him."*

One of the easiest ways I know to go broke is to try to make a lot of money quickly. I will let you in on a little secret. If there were an honest and easy way to make a lot of money fast, we are too late to discover it. Something in our lazy, wicked flesh is always looking for an easy way. God told Adam, "In the sweat of thy face shalt thou eat bread" (Genesis 3:19). And we think that with just a little effort we'll build granaries full of wheat for bread for the years ahead. A person that hastens to be rich doesn't even think right.

The world has all kinds of get-rich-quick schemes. Somebody had one in a magazine not too many years ago that read, "Send $10 for a guaranteed way to make $10,000." Everyone that sent $10 to that address got a note saying, "Put an ad in the magazine and hope that there are a 1,000 suckers just like you out there." Get-rich-quick schemes are really get-poor-quick schemes. Many a person has followed one form or another thinking that it was within their grasp to have riches quickly.

Proverbs 13:7a says,

> *"There is that maketh himself rich, yet hath nothing...."*

Read the stories of the lives of most of those that had a get-rich-quick scheme, and see how broke they were when they died. They acquired it, and then lost it just as quickly. The principle God lays down here is this: A quick success usually leads to a quick failure. You don't value it because you got it quickly, and it will be gone just as quickly. Some of you have been around long enough to see people who have jumped into such, and seemed to prosper. They told how great it was. In some cases, it wasn't ten years before they were looking for some way to get started again or to recover themselves. It is amazing how the people got so rich in the late 20's on the stock market and lost it all overnight. Some others that had labored and worked and didn't have nearly as much, were in better shape when the stock market went broke and the banks went under.

Another Scripture on this matter is Proverbs 15:27a,

> **"He that is greedy of gain troubleth his own house ..."**

Observe also that those that are always trying to get rich quick, never have peace in their home. If their marriage doesn't end in divorce, there will at least be misery in the relationship. They have forgotten that their home is of greater value. I am not talking about the building, but rather the relationship. Money won't replace it. Some of the most miserable people that I know are some of the wealthiest I have ever met. They have gone for the money and lost what is valuable in life.

Proverbs 21:5 says,

> *"The thoughts of the diligent tend only to plenteousness; but of every one that is hasty only to want."*

If a man is diligent in his thinking, he is simply going to stick with it, laboring, and working. The result is that he will have plenty. If his thoughts are always to being hasty to get wealth, the result is that he will be poor. Get-rich-quick thinking is

CHAPTER 24: GET RICH QUICK SCHEMES

unbiblical and an unreal thought pattern. Somehow, they think they can shortcut the system and that they are wise and everyone else is a fool. Consequently, they look down on others and see people as instruments and tools to be used. Before long they find out, they are the losers.

Proverbs 28:20 tells us,

> *"A faithful man shall abound with blessings; but he that maketh haste to be rich shall not be innocent."*

In their hurry to get-rich-quick, it is not long before such individuals' actions are wrong. They will twist the truth a little, cheat a little on their taxes, manipulate, take advantage, etc. God says, any one that is in a hurry to get rich "shall not be innocent". Then just two verses later, the Scripture states that poverty shall come upon him. It is a curse for people to think that they are going to get rich quick and easy. They have forgotten that it is "easy come and easy go."

WHAT IS THE CURE?

Get rich slowly. Take your time at it. Work hard and long. Be diligent and frugal. Be careful. Invest. Work hard and long. Be patient. Live below your means. Work hard. Work long. Be diligent. Be patient. Keep working and investing. Learn. Keep working hard and long. Be patient ... and on it goes.

God says that the other way won't pay. Learn to plan for the long run. Think in terms of what you are going to do between now and death, if you have a normal life. If you think God might let you have five more years then figure on a five-year plan. Start figuring on that basis instead of planning to have it all by the first of the year. If you get it all, the government will take half of it anyway. Wouldn't it be better to earn it slowly and pay a low tax rate than to earn it fast and have to give most of it up? Even the government will try to teach us that lesson.

CHAPTER 25

CONCLUSION

Somehow, we must get our thinking re-oriented. We need to realize also that wealth should never be a goal, but only a tool for the real goals of life. What do you want that money for anyway? To leave it to someone who won't appreciate it?

I have previously mentioned the man I worked with in the shoe store being such a miser. He wouldn't take a lunch break, but instead would eat a peanut butter and jelly sandwich while he was finding shoes for a customer. He wouldn't miss a customer for anything. The store manager would make him take a two week vacation and if he stayed away for most of a week, they were thrilled. He would read a newspaper that he had picked up on the bus seat coming in to work while he left his brand new car sitting in the garage at home, because it was cheaper to come that way. He didn't have a telephone. He hoped to be able to get by without using light bulbs because they lasted longer that way and he didn't pay much of an electric bill. That is just the way he was.

I asked him one day what he was going to do with all that money. He said that he was just gathering it up. When I asked him what for, he said that he was going to leave it for the people left behind. I asked him if he had any children, and he told me he didn't. So then I asked what his beneficiaries were going to do with his money, and he said that he hadn't thought about that but he supposed they were going to fight over it and waste it all. I inquired, "That is what you're spending your whole life on?" His reply was, "That's right." I asked him if he had ever thought about that and he said. "I don't want to think about that, but here comes a customer, and I am going to sell another pair of shoes."

His goal was wealth.

We must learn that wealth is a tool, and there is nothing wrong with it, if it is used correctly. David got wealth, but he wanted to build a temple for God. God told him to just get the money together and He would let his son build it. Solomon had it built in great splendor and glory. Some women had money and financed the work of Jesus. They ministered to Him financially during that time. They learned that it is a tool, not a goal in life. It is a means for getting on through life.

You don't live to get rich. However, if you can obtain and gather some material for a heritage and inheritance for your children, that is good and Biblical, if it helps them to do more for God in the days ahead. To be able to make provision is right. After all, God made provision for us, didn't He? You may say that maybe some people's children wouldn't be worthy. How worthy were we of all the provision that God made? If you were going to make it on the basis of worth, He would have been better to keep Jesus in heaven. I want you to know He made a tremendous investment for us. In fact, the mansions are already built. The Bible says, "In my Father's house are many mansions …" (John 14:2a). I am not going to heaven to occupy a mansion; I am going to see Jesus. I just have that mansion while I am there – that is all. You see, wealth is a tool; it is not the main purpose of life. Those that will live for money don't have much to live for.

There is no need for us to be making ourselves as poor as we do so often.

"The righteous considereth the cause of the poor." (**Proverbs 29:7**).

We should consider the cause of our own poverty, shouldn't we? Consider it and do something about it. There are cures.

CHAPTER 25: CONCLUSION

There is some deliverance. God's work could do far more if we weren't so bound up financially. It may take a generation or most of a lifetime for some to get straightened out, but if their children are saved, they will have a start and be able to do more. What if Jesus comes back? We will be walking in the light of the Word of God. There are going to be people saved that didn't have Christian parents. Thus, there is always going to be a need for you to know these Christian principles to help them begin to get out of their financial ruin.

There is going to be a bigger need in the future to get back to the Biblical principles because the world has lost sight of them. We need to be teaching them because here is where they started – with God.

Proverbs 29:7

"The righteous considereth the cause of the poor: but the wicked regardeth not to know it."

CAUSES AND CURES OF POVERTY

INDEX OF WORDS AND PHRASES

accountant, 82
advertising, 64, 75
alabaster box, 10
ambassador, 78
amusement, 75, 84, 94
Ananias, 36
ant, 78
Apostle John, 9
authority of the Word of God, 99
babbling, 50
bank, 15, 17, 23, 25, 81, 82, 83, 84, 85, 96
bankruptcy, 85
Barnum and Bailey Circus, 75
Bible Institute, 60
Biblical principle, 12, 41, 67, 109
blackmail, 28
Bob Doom, 61
bondage, 81, 83
borrower, 81, 84
Borrowing money, 81
Caesars, 32
Caleb, 69
capitalistic society, 18
cathedral-like churches, 31
cause of the poor, 15, 84, 108, 109
checkbooks, 37
chintzy, 60
cold, 65, 94
college, 7, 11, 25, 45, 46
conceit, 68, 69
conscious effort, 24
content, 13
Count the cost, 26
court, 27, 68, 85, 86
cure, 15, 16, 17, 19, 22, 29, 32, 35, 38, 42, 44, 50, 71, 85
dabble, 97

Dad, 44
David, 11, 32, 68, 108
deer, 64
defense, 39, 40
depression, 16
Devil, 23, 38, 72
Diligence, 35
Disasters, 10
Disney World, 95
documents, 87
drunk, 93, 94, 95, 96, 100
drunkard, 24, 93, 96, 100
dwarf, 75
earthquakes, 10
easy job, 65
eat, 13, 41, 56, 57, 73, 76, 100, 102, 103, 107
Ecclesiastes, 14
escape mechanism, 24
evil men, 77
farmer, 37, 40, 55, 57, 67, 92, 101
farmers, 10
feasting, 99, 100
finance, 13, 85
financial condition, 16
financial mess, 16
financial philosophy, 16
flattery, 43
food, 13, 60, 61, 68, 81, 99, 100
friends, 95, 101, 102
frugality, 60
Gaius, 9
Gambling, 93
gardens, 41
gathereth by labour, 43, 44
get our thinking re-oriented, 107
get-rich-quick schemes, 103
gift of gab, 54

gifts, 89, 91
glory to a person, 47
glory to God, 47
gluttony, 99, 100
go out and work, 44
Goliath, 68
Gomorrah, 29, 71
government that will encourage wickedness, 32
grandchildren, 65
greedy, 21, 22, 104
hammer, 46
hand of the diligent maketh rich, 35
hardware store, 46, 55
help someone, 16
high expense of traveling, 25
honest, 21, 22, 29, 99, 103
honeycomb, 28
idleness, 63, 64, 72
ignorant, 50
ignorantly, 11
immorally, 27, 29
instruction, 4, 49, 50, 66, 67
Israelites, 69
Joshua, 69
lay plans, 38
lazy, 46, 59, 63, 103
Learn to be accountable, 37
learning to be content, 13
life is a game, 76
lion, 67, 68, 69
lips, 28, 53, 54
Liquor, 93
Loose living, 27
love of pleasure, 75
machine, 53, 55
Malachi, 41
Manhattan Island, 87
manipulated legally, 87
marks of the righteous, 15
measures of revival, 17
millennium, 12
million dollars, 18, 19, 84, 115

minimum wage, 12
ministry, 54, 115
miser, 107
missionaries, 38, 78
missionary, 11
moral integrity, 21
multitude of counsellors, 50
oats, 28, 67
opossum, 69
oppressing the poor, 88, 91
pay, 11, 15, 22, 25, 28, 45, 46, 51, 55, 56, 57, 67, 78, 81, 82, 83, 85, 88, 91, 92, 100, 105, 107
paycheck, 11, 27
Penury, 53
Peter, 78
Pharaohs, 32
philosophies of man, 18
piece of paper, 36
piling up his money, 31
Pinhook Hollow, 94
pleasures, 75, 76, 94, 96, 100
poor, 9, 10, 12, 13, 15, 17, 21, 24, 25, 32, 35, 37, 39, 43, 44, 49, 50, 59, 71, 72, 75, 78, 81, 83, 84, 87, 88, 89, 91, 92, 95, 96, 103, 104, 108
Poverty, 4, 9, 12, 19, 49
pray, 14, 38
preaching, 16, 17, 54, 75, 95
professor, 25, 96
prosper, 9, 14, 38, 104
protection, 39, 40
rabbit, 64
receivership, 84
recession, 16, 45
recycling, 60
Red Sea, 69
repentance, 85
reproof, 4, 49, 50
Rescue Mission, 60
restitution, 85
rich, 9, 13, 14, 17, 19, 32, 39, 40,

INDEX OF WORDS AND PHRASES

49, 66, 75, 78, 81, 83, 87, 88, 91, 92, 96, 103, 104, 105, 108
rich get richer, 83
righteous, 15, 31, 32, 84, 108, 109
Righteousness is the cure, 33
Riley, 93
Roman Catholic church, 31
salesman, 21, 53
Sapphira, 36
Satan, 11, 36
Saul, 68
save, 13, 14, 18, 25, 79, 83, 86
sawdust, 67
scattereth yet increaseth, 42
seducers, 77
servant to the lender, 81, 84
Shakespeare, 76
shepherd, 44, 68
Shoddy workmanship, 22
shoes, 107
Siamese twins, 75
Sinking Springs, 94
slavery, 81, 82, 83, 84
sleep, 23, 24, 63, 100
slothful, 59, 63, 64, 65, 66, 67, 68, 69, 76
Slothfulness, 59, 63
sluggard, 64, 65, 68, 69, 78
Sodom, 29, 71, 72
sodomy, 29
soil, 55
Solomon, 11, 14, 108
spend less, 79
spiritual issue, 9
steal, 13
Steven Worth, 79
stinginess in giving, 41
styles of government, 18
sweat, 53, 54, 68, 103
sweet talker, 28
sword, 28, 75
taxes, 78, 94, 105
tempt God, 36

the sense of a bird, 21
toil, 53, 54
Tom Riley, 94
Traveling, 25
treasures, 32, 42
treasures of wickedness profit nothing, 32
two nickels to rub, 11
U.S Post Office, 56
unemployment, 56, 57
vanity, 13, 43, 44
vehicle, 25
Vietnam, 40
Volkswagen, 25
vows of poverty, 11
Wall Street Journal, 13
wanting, 40, 64, 66
wanting, but not doing, 66
waste, 10, 38, 60, 102, 107
Wastefulness, 59
wealthy, 17, 31, 32, 35, 87
Weather, 10
weeds, 37
widows, 44, 46
wrong way to make money, 43

FOR YOUR PERSONAL NOTES

ABOUT THE AUTHOR

J. PAUL RENO has been a pastor in Ohio and Maryland since 1968. During this time he has also been involved in church planting, training men for the ministry and speaking on mission fields in Europe, the Middle East, Africa, South America and Mexico. The church he presently pastors has just passed sending 3 and 2/3 million dollars to missions. He continues to speak at various Bible conferences, camp meetings and local churches. He presently serves on the Board of Directors for the Conversion Center, which is headquartered in Hagerstown, Maryland. Pastor Reno recently was honored with the prestigious award, "Defender of the Scriptures," by the King James Bible Research Council.

He is also the author of *To Fight or Not to Fight*, *Daniel Nash: Prevailing Prince of Prayer*, *Investing for Eternity*, *Studies in Bible Doctrine* as well as over fifty pamphlets and booklets on salvation, the Christian life, Bible doctrine and the King James Version. His wife, Carolyn authored *Almost But Lost*, available as a free ebook download at:

http://www.theoldpathspublications.com/Pages/Free.htm.